Business English

Book 1

John Taylor
Jeff Zeter

Express Publishing

Table of Contents

Greetings and goodbyes

greet

Get ready!

1 Before you read the passage, talk about these questions.

1 What do you say and do when you meet a friend?

2 Do people kiss when they greet in your country? What do you think of this?

Reading

2 🎧 **Listen and read this extract from an etiquette guide. Then, choose the correct answers. How many customs are mentioned in the text?**

1 Which is NOT a common way of greeting mentioned in the guide?

   A saying 'Pleased to meet you'

   B kissing each other's hands

   C bowing

   D shaking hands

2 How does the guide suggest people react when they experience a new greeting?

   A shake hands firmly

   B be polite

   C use your best judgment

   D follow local customs

3 What can you guess about people in Saudi Arabia?

   A They use a firm handshake.

   B They say goodbye with a kiss.

   C They don't typically bow when greeting.

   D They have similar customs to Europeans.

Vocabulary

3 Complete the word or phrase with the same meaning as the underlined part.

1 The manager said, '<u>I am happy to see you</u>'.
   P _ e _ _ _ _   _ o   _ e _ t   _ _ u

2 Be polite when you <u>meet and say hello to</u> a client.
   g _ _ e _

3 Some people kiss on the <u>side of the face</u>.
   _ h _ e _

4 It was <u>good to see and get to know you</u>.
   n _ _ _   _ e _ t _ _ _   _ o _

Page 12

Everyone's Business: Issue 344

Etiquette

People around the world say hello and goodbye in different ways. In Asia, many people **bow** when they **greet** each other. This might seem strange to someone in the Middle East. There, men sometimes greet each other with a **kiss** on the **cheek**. In most countries, people **shake hands**. But in America and Europe the handshake is **firm**, while in Asia it is often soft. So what do you do when you meet people from other countries? Don't let these **customs** confuse you. Just be **polite**. When you meet, say '**Pleased to meet you**' and ask 'How are you?' When it is time to leave, say '**It was nice meeting you**' and 'I hope we meet again.'

4 **Read the sentence pairs. Choose where the words best fit in the blanks.**

1 **bow / customs**

Most nations have different _____ for greeting strangers.

Japanese businessmen often _____ to each other.

2 **kiss / shake hands**

Some people don't _____ unless they are in a romantic relationship.

Business people often _____ when they come to an agreement.

3 **polite / firm**

Be _____ when meeting new people.

In America, a _____ handshake shows a strong personality.

Listening

5 🎧 **Listen to a conversation between a manager and his colleague. Mark the following statements as true (T) or false (F).**

1 __ The manager advises his colleague to bow.

2 __ The manager advises his colleague to shake hands softly.

3 __ The manager suggests shaking hands with Mr. Yakamoto.

6 🎧 **Listen again and complete the conversation.**

Manager:	When you meet Mr. Yakamoto, be very **1** _____ . He is a very important client.
Colleague:	It's the Japanese **2** _____ to bow. Should I do that?
Manager:	No, you don't have to bow. Just say '**3** _____ _____ meet you' and **4** _____ _____ .
Colleague:	Okay.
Manager:	But don't make your handshake too **5** _____ . Japanese people usually have a softer handshake.
Colleague:	And when he leaves? What then?
Manager:	Just say 'It was **6** _____ _____ _____ ' and shake his hand again.
Colleague:	Okay, that's fine!

Speaking

7 **With a partner, act out the roles below, based on the dialogue from Task 6. Then switch roles.**

USE LANGUAGE SUCH AS:

You must be polite.

It is the custom to …

Don't make your handshake too firm.

Student A: Give advice to your colleague about how to:
- greet a client
- shake hands
- say goodbye

Make up a client's name and nationality

Student B: You are meeting a client from another country. Ask Student A for advice about greetings.

Writing

8 **Use the conversation from Task 7 to complete the memo.**

Uniworks
Employee Manual

5.54 ▾ GREETING CLIENTS

When greeting clients, you must always _____

With American clients, _____

With Japanese clients, _____

When you greet the client, say _____

When the client leaves, say _____ and _____

5

Let me introduce you to ...

left out

Page 18

Everyone's Business: Issue 344

Introduction Etiquette

Imagine you are at a conference, talking to a **colleague**. Suddenly an old friend greets you. Of course you are happy to see him and you start talking excitedly. Stop! What about your colleague? Don't leave her alone. **Introduce** your friend and colleague by saying "I'd like you to meet ..." or "**Let me introduce you to ...**" Make sure each person understands your **relationship** with the other, and **mention** each person's **occupation**. Think of something the two have **in common** and **steer the conversation** in that direction. This way, neither of them will feel **left out**.

Get ready!

1 Before you read the passage, talk about these questions.

1 What are some situations in which you have to introduce people?

2 What are the differences between good and bad introductions?

Reading

2 Read this extract from an etiquette guide, then mark the following statements as true (T) or false (F).

1 ___ End a conversation with a colleague before talking to friend.

2 ___ Do not talk about work when introducing two people.

3 ___ Mentioning people's common interest makes them feel included.

Vocabulary

3 Choose the word that is closest in meaning to the underlined part.

1 James likes to talk about his job.
   A relationship
   B colleague
   C occupation

2 Change the topic away from politics.
   A mention
   B steer the conversation
   C introduce

3 Karen is talking to a person with whom she works.
   A colleague
   B relationship
   C occupation

4 Let me tell you the name of my friend, Bob Hawkins.
   A steer the conversation away from
   B leave out
   C introduce you to

4 **Place a check (✓) next to the response that answers the question.**

1 Have I met your friend before?
   A __ No. Mary, _I'd like you to meet_ Polly.
   B __ Yes. My friend Polly feels _left out_.

2 What's your _relationship_ with Helen?
   A __ She didn't _mention_ your name.
   B __ She's my _colleague_.

3 Can I _introduce_ you to my colleague, Daniel?
   A __ Sure! _Nice to meet you_ Daniel.
   B __ Don't mention it.

5 🎧 **Listen and read the extract again. How should you introduce a colleague to an old friend?**

Listening

6 🎧 **Listen to a conversation between two men and a woman. Mark the following statements as true (T) or false (F).**

1 __ The woman is introduced to the friend of a colleague.

2 __ The speakers are at the woman's birthday party.

3 __ All three speakers are in the same soccer league.

7 🎧 **Listen again and complete the conversation.**

Man 1:	Sarah, I'd like you to meet **1** _____ _____, John. John, this is Sarah.
Woman:	Hi John, it's a pleasure to meet you.
Man 2:	And nice to meet you, too. How do you two know **2** _____ _____?
Woman:	Oh, we work together.
Man 2:	That's right. Bob mentioned that some of his colleagues were coming to **3** _____ _____ party.
Man 1:	You know, Sarah, you and John have something **4** _____ _____ .
Woman:	**5** _____? What's that?
Man 1:	**6** _____ _____ in the same adult soccer league.

Speaking

8 **In groups of three, act out the roles below, based on the dialogue from Task 7. Then switch roles.**

USE LANGUAGE SUCH AS:

I'd like you to meet …

How do you two know one another?

You and … have something in common.

Student A: Introduce two people who do not know each other. Be sure to mention:
- names
- similar interests

Make up some names and an interest.

Student B and C: Greet the person you are introduced to. Find out:
- how he or she knows Student A

Writing

9 **Use the conversation from Task 8 and the etiquette guide to fill out the journal entry. Use today's date.**

Date _____

Today, I went to _____

While I was there, I met _____

S/He works with _____

We have something in common. We _____
_____

Hopefully, we'll meet again.

Get ready!

1 **Before you read the passage, talk about these questions.**

1 What do you talk about with someone you don't know well?

2 What do you do when a conversation is going poorly?

Small Talk
By Hugh Trenchard

It happens to everyone. Somebody introduces you to a friend and then walks away. Now you're standing with somebody you don't know. What do you talk about?

The **weather** is always a possibility. But there isn't always much to say. To make a conversation **flow**, it's better to ask questions. Ask the other person what they do for a **living**, and what their job **involves**. **Discussing** your own former jobs is a good option, too.

Other safe **topics** include your home town and your education. But **avoid** asking people about their **religion**, age and **marital status** until you know them better.

Reading

2 **Read this extract from a blog, then complete the table using information from the passage.**

When talking to someone you don't know …	
talk about …	1 _____
ask about …	2 _____ what their job involves
discuss …	jobs you did in the past 3 _____ 4 _____
don't talk about …	religion 5 _____ marital status

Vocabulary

3 **Fill in the blanks with the correct words from the word bank.**

WORD BANK

avoid   **discuss**   flow   involves   **living**

1 What does Heidi do for a _____?

2 Graham's job _____ buying supplies.

3 _____ personal topics with strangers.

4 Helen's conversation with Rick didn't _____ .

5 Fiona chose not to _____ religion with clients.

4 Match the words (1-5) with the definitions (A-E).

1 __ small talk   4 __ religion
2 __ weather   5 __ marital status
3 __ topic

A a polite conversation about everyday things
B a belief or worship of a god or gods
C the temperature, rain, clouds and wind
D the condition of either being married or single
E a subject for conversation or study

5 🎧 Listen and read the blog extract. again. What is the best way to make a conversation flow?

Listening

6 🎧 Listen to a conversation between a businessman and a colleague. Check (✓) the topics that are suggested to talk about.

1 ☐ age   4 ☐ weather
2 ☐ work   5 ☐ marital status
3 ☐ religion   6 ☐ education

7 🎧 Listen again and complete the conversation.

Businessman:	Sarah, I have to take a phone call. Please make 1 _____ _____ with Mr. Jensen until I'm free.
Colleague:	But I don't know him! I have nothing to talk to him about.
Businessman:	Just ask him what he does for a 2 _____ .
Colleague:	But I already know what his work 3 _____ . After all, he's our consultant.
Businessman:	Then why don't you 4 _____ the weather?
Colleague:	It's not a very interesting 5 _____ .
Businessman:	Well, I'm sure you'll think of something. Just don't bring up his 6 _____ _____ .
Colleague:	Good to know, thanks.

Speaking

8 With a partner, act out the roles below, based on the dialogue from Task 7. Then switch roles.

USE LANGUAGE SUCH AS:

Can you make small talk with ...?
Why don't you discuss ...?
Avoid talking about ...

Student A: You cannot meet with a client. Ask Student B to make small talk. Suggest:
● topics to discuss
● topics to avoid
Make up a name for your client and your employee.

Student B: Your boss wants you to make small talk with a client. Ask what to talk about.

Writing

9 Use the conversation from Task 8 and the blog extract to fill out the email.

■ ■ ■
Dear ___ ,
You said you are worried about making small talk in your new job. Here are some ideas.
Ask lots of questions because _____ .
Ask questions about _____ .
You could also discuss _____ .
Avoid talking about _____ .
At least until _____ .
Hope this helps!

Angie's Advice
by: Angie Andrews

Dear Chatty Colleague,

Everyone has a colleague that can talk too much. These "little chats" can **take up** a lot of **time**. It is always hard to end the conversation without being **rude**, but there are some things you can do to improve the situation. Here are some polite **phrases** to help you in the future.

● Anyway, I'd better **run**.

● I should **get back** to work now.

● **I'm afraid** I'm very busy at the moment. Can we talk later?

● Unfortunately, I don't **have the time**.

All these phrases signal the end of a conversation, so hopefully your talkative co-worker will let you return to work. Remember to always keep a polite **tone**, so you don't cause **hurt feelings**. Good luck!

Get ready!

❶ Before you read the passage, talk about these questions.

1 When might you have to end a conversation before someone has finished talking?

2 What are some phrases people can use to end a conversation politely?

Reading

❷ 🎧 Listen and read this excerpt from an advice column. Then, choose the correct answers. How many ways does it give to end a conversation?

1 What is the main idea of the advice column?
   A how to politely exit a conversation
   B the proper time for certain conversations
   C ways to improve conversations with co-workers
   D types of conversations not to have at work

2 According to the passage, what action will prevent a co-worker from feeling bad?
   A returning to work
   B talking to someone later
   C speaking in the correct tone
   D ending a conversation quickly

3 According to the passage, which is NOT true?
   A Small talk at work can cost a lot of time.
   B Ending a conversation can cause hurt feelings.
   C Most offices have a person who talks a lot.
   D It is rude to end a conversation with a co-worker.

Vocabulary

❸ Write a word that is similar in meaning to the underlined part.

1 The salesman was impolite and unfriendly.
   _ _ _ e

2 John needs to return to work.
   _ _ _   _ a _ _

3 Patrick should leave now or he will be late.
   b _ _ t _ _   _ _ n

4 Knowing a few foreign groups of words is useful when traveling.
   p _ _ _ _ _ s

5 Too much conversation at work uses a lot of time.
   _ _ _ e _   _ _

4 **Fill in the blanks with the correct words and phrases from the word bank.**

word BANK

busy   tone   hurt someone's feelings
unfortunately   afraid   have a lot of time

1 _____, Jim will not be attending the meeting.

2 Ms. Baker isn't polite and is going to _____ .

3 The businessmen _____ because their plane is late.

4 The office is _____ since there are many people working.

5 Mr. Fox is _____ that he'll be late.

6 Use the right _____ of voice in work conversations.

Listening

5 🎧 **Listen to a conversation between two colleagues. Mark the following statements as true (T) or false (F).**

1 __ The man recently took a trip.

2 __ The woman tries to end the conversation.

3 __ The speakers plan to talk the next day.

6 🎧 **Listen again and complete the conversation.**

Colleague 1:	Hey John! How are you? How was your 1 _____?
Colleague 2:	Oh, hi Susan. It was wonderful. Aruba is 2 _____ .
Colleague 1:	Wow! I want to go to the Caribbean. Was the weather nice?
Colleague 2:	Yes, the weather was fantastic. And the people are very 3 _____ .
Colleague 1:	Great. Tell me more. Was it 4 _____?
Colleague 2:	Well, I'm afraid I'm really busy at the moment. Can we talk 5 _____ _____?
Colleague 1:	Sure, no 6 _____ .
Colleague 2:	Okay. See you then.

Speaking

7 **With a partner, act out the roles below, based on the dialogue from Task 6. Use your own names. Then switch roles.**

USE LANGUAGE SUCH AS:

How was your ...?

I'm afraid ...

Can we talk later?

Student A: You work with Student B. Talk to him or her about:

● a vacation

● weather

● expenses

Make up a destination for your vacation.

Student B: Answers Student A's questions and politely end the conversation.

Writing

8 **Use the conversation from Task 7 and the excerpt to complete the email.**

Hi _____,

Sorry to hear so many people are bothering you at work. If I were you, I'd just end the conversation early. After you _____ .
_____ , just say _____
Or you could ask _____ .

That's my advice. Hope it helps!

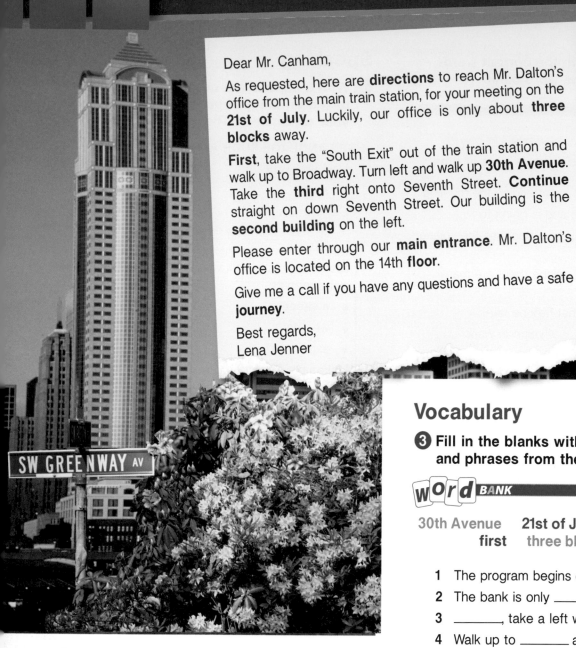

Dear Mr. Canham,

As requested, here are **directions** to reach Mr. Dalton's office from the main train station, for your meeting on the **21st of July**. Luckily, our office is only about **three blocks** away.

First, take the "South Exit" out of the train station and walk up to Broadway. Turn left and walk up **30th Avenue**. Take the **third** right onto Seventh Street. **Continue** straight on down Seventh Street. Our building is the **second building** on the left.

Please enter through our **main entrance**. Mr. Dalton's office is located on the 14th **floor**.

Give me a call if you have any questions and have a safe **journey**.

Best regards,
Lena Jenner

Get ready!

❶ **Before you read the passage, talk about these questions.**

1   What kind of errors occur when ordering numbers?

2   Why are numbers so important when giving directions?

Reading

❷ **Read the letter, then mark the following statements as true (T) or false (F).**

1 __ Mr. Canham is taking the train to the office.

2 __ Mr. Canham is going to visit Ms. Jenner.

3 __ The office is located on Seventh Street.

Vocabulary

❸ **Fill in the blanks with the correct words and phrases from the word bank.**

wO**rd** BANK

30th Avenue	**21st of July**	second building
first	**three blocks**	floor

1   The program begins on the _____ .

2   The bank is only _____ away from here.

3   _____, take a left when exiting the building.

4   Walk up to _____ and take a right turn.

5   The opera house is the _____ on your left.

6   You can purchase tickets on the first _____ .

❹ **Place a check (✓) next to the response that correctly answers the question.**

1   Does Ms. Canham need <u>directions</u> to the bank?

   A __ No, she goes there every day.

   B __ Yes, she lives two blocks away.

2   How long was the <u>journey</u>?

   A __ It's located on the fourth floor.

   B __ It was over two hundred miles.

3   Do we have to enter through the <u>main entrance</u>?

   A __ No, it's on the 22rd of May.

   B __ Yes, it's the only way in or out.

5 🎧 Listen and read the letter again. What should Mr. Canham do if he has a problem?

Listening

6 🎧 Listen to a conversation between a receptionist and a client. Choose the correct answers.

1 What is the main purpose of the call?

   A to confirm an appointment

   B to request instructions

   C to correct a mistake

   D to change a meeting time

2 Which building is Mr. Dalton's office in?

   A the fourth

   B the second

   C the twenty-first

   D the first

7 🎧 Listen again and complete the conversation.

Client:	Hillson and Sons. Mr. Canham **1** _____ . How can I help you?
Receptionist:	Hi, Mr. Canham. **2** _____ Lena from Mr. Dalton's office.
Client:	Oh, hi Lena. How are you?
Receptionist:	I'm well, thanks. I'm **3** _____ calling about your visit on July **4** _____ .
Client:	Yes, I received your **5** _____ yesterday.
Receptionist:	Oh, good. Well, I'm afraid there's a **6** _____ . Our building is actually the fourth building on the left, not the second.
Client:	Okay. Let me make a note of that. Anything else?
Receptionist:	No. That's everything.

Speaking

8 With a partner, act out the roles below, based on the dialogue from Task 6. Then switch roles.

USE LANGUAGE SUCH AS:

How can I help you?

I'm calling about …

Let me make a note of that.

Student A: You want to give directions to your office for an appointment. Talk to Student B about

● the date

● directions

Make up a date for your meeting.

Student B: You are a client of Student A's business. Get directions.

Writing

9 Use the conversation from Task 7 and the letter to complete the directions.

Date of meeting: _____

Directions to the office: _____

_____

_____

_____

_____

_____

Office floor #: _____

Staff,

As you know, our sales **figures** this year are very low. Our sales in Europe fell by 13 **percent** in the last **quarter**, which is the biggest **percentage** fall ever.

Our sales are only $1.34 billion, to be exact. The recent financial crisis was very bad. First, we lost a huge **fraction** of our business – **approximately** 1/6 of our Asian clients. Second, our national **currency** lost value; the Euro is now stronger than the dollar.

Fortunately, the experts **forecast** some good figures. They **estimate** a 3% increase in sales by the end of next year. Still, we'll need to double that in order to make up what we lost last year.

Get ready!

❶ **Before you read the passage, talk about these questions.**

1 What are some different ways to express numbers and figures?

2 What are the consequences of mistakes in figures?

Reading

❷ 🎧 **Listen and read this excerpt from a business memo. Then, choose the correct answers. How much do they need to increase their sales by to reach the level of sales in the previous year?**

1 What is the business report mostly about?
   A poor sales figures
   B a strategy to increase sales
   C reasons the staff is being reduced
   D how to increase the number of clients

2 What can be inferred about the company?
   A It does most of its business in Asia.
   B It earned more than $1 billion last year.
   C It is forecasted to double its sales next year.
   D It estimates that the Euro will lose value.

3 Which is NOT a problem for the company?
   A their currency
   B the Asian market
   C the sales forecast
   D their sales figures

Vocabulary

❸ **Choose the word that is closest in meaning to the underlined part.**

1 The boss wants the <u>official numbers</u> in a report today.
   A figures   B currency   C forecast

2 The worst time was the last <u>three months</u> of the year.
   A percentage   B forecast   C quarter

3 Many countries use their own <u>form of money</u>.
   A fraction   B currency   C percentage

4 Read the sentence pairs. Choose where the words best fit in the blanks.

1 **fraction / percent**

The firm's market share increased by fifteen _____ .

The business lost a small _____ of its clients.

2 **Forecast / Estimate**

_____ the sales for next year.

Ms. Elm can only _____ the cost, she doesn't know it exactly.

3 **exact / approximately**

The sales figures for this year are _____ $1 million.

Get the _____ figure, not a guess.

Listening

5 🎧 Listen to a telephone conversation between two colleagues. Mark the following statements as true (T) or false (F).

1 __ The man called to confirm the results of a report.

2 __ The woman has not completed the report yet.

3 __ The company's market share increased.

6 🎧 Listen again and complete the conversation.

Colleague 1: Hello.

Colleague 2: Hello, Phyllis. Lucas **1** _____ .

Colleague 1: Oh, hi Lucas. What can I do for you?

Colleague 2: I'm actually calling about your sales report for the **2** _____ . Is it ready?

Colleague 1: Almost, I'll finish it later today. I can send it to you by this **3** _____ .

Colleague 2: Great. How about the **4** _____? Do they look good?

Colleague 1: Amazing! Our sales figures are better than **5** _____ . And our market share is 3 percent **6** _____ than last quarter.

Colleague 2: Wow! That is great news.

Speaking

7 With a partner, act out the roles below, based on the dialogue from Task 6. Then switch roles.

USE LANGUAGE SUCH AS:

I'm actually calling about …

I can send it to you by …

How about the results?

Student A: Call one of your employees to ask about a sales report. Talk to Student B about:

● the report

● if it is complete

● the results

Student B: Your boss calls you to find out about a sales report. Create figures and tell Student A about:

● status of the report

● sales figures

● market share

Writing

8 Use the conversation from Task 7 and the excerpt from the memo to complete the notes.

Bentley's Sales Department

Name of salesperson: _____

Report Complete? Y / N

Due date: _____

Sales results for the quarter:

Sales figures _____

Market share _____

How to Stay Organized

You lead a busy life, and time is very valuable to you. The key to your success is effective scheduling!

- Your **schedule** is the most important thing in your business life. Use one that you can keep with you all the time. For example, a paper **diary** or **electronic planner** – NOT a wall **calendar**!

- Keep your schedule **up-to-date**. Suppose your client calls and cancels an **appointment**. **Erase** it immediately. Or your client makes a new appointment on June 23rd. Enter it right then.

- At the beginning of each month, check your schedule for **deadlines**. Then, make a 'to-do' list in order of **priority**.

- Finally, don't forget to **schedule** time off! Everybody needs to relax. Enjoying your free time gives you more energy for business success!

Get ready!

1 Before you read the passage, talk about these questions.

1 How does technology help people stay organized?

2 Have you ever forgotten about an appointment? How did it happen?

Reading

2 🎧 Listen and read this blog entry. Then, choose the correct answers. How can you make yourself more successful in business?

1 What is the purpose of the guide?

   A to advise people how to use their free time

   B to help people plan and use time effectively

   C to explain the functions of electronic planners

   D to compare the effectiveness of diaries and planners

2 What should you do when informed that a client will not attend a meeting?

   A set a deadline for a new one

   B remove it from your planner

   C schedule a new one immediately

   D add a new meeting to your to-do list

3 What should you do at the start of a new month?

   A enter all new appointment times

   B arrange relaxation in your free time

   C erase deadlines that have been met

   D schedule tasks in order of importance

Vocabulary

3 Match the words (1-6) with the definitions (A-F).

1 __ schedule   4 __ erase

2 __ diary   5 __ enter

3 __ appointment   6 __ deadline

A the date or time by which something must be finished

B a book with spaces for a year's days, weeks and months

C to remove something

D to add something

E a plan of events and the times they will happen

F an arrangement to meet at a particular time

4 Fill in the blanks with the correct words and phrases from the word bank.

word BANK

up-to-date   calendar   schedule
priority   electronic planner

1 The _____ on the wall shows what day it is.

2 Simone is _____ on the recent trends.

3 Finish the highest _____ tasks before less important ones.

4 David uses a(n) _____ so that he has his plans with him at all times.

5 The managers want to _____ the meeting for ten o'clock.

Listening

5 🎧 Listen to a conversation between two business people. Mark the following statements as true (T) or false (F).

1 __ The man is calling to confirm an appointment.

2 __ The woman is not available on the 21st of June.

3 __ The speakers will meet at 12:00 on the 27th.

6 🎧 Listen again and complete the conversation.

Man: Hi Sandra, it's Mark.

Woman: Hi Mark, how can I help you?

Man: Well, I'm really sorry, but I need to **1** _____ our appointment on the 21st.

Woman: Oh, that's okay. Do you want to **2** _____?

Man: That'd be great. Are you **3** _____ on the 27th of June?

Woman: Let me see. Yes, I am. How does noon **4** _____?

Man: That's **5** _____ . Thank you very much.

Woman: No **6** _____ . See you then.

Speaking

7 With a partner, act out the roles below, based on the dialogue from Task 6. Then switch roles.

USE LANGUAGE SUCH AS:

Do you want to reschedule?

Are you free on the …

Do you want to meet on the …

Student A: Call an associate about an appointment. Talk to Student B about:
● cancelling
● rescheduling
● time
Make up a time and date for a new appointment

Student B: Arrange a new appointment with Student A.

Writing

8 Use this schedule to plan your appointments and deadlines for this week.

Weekly Planner

	Mon	Tues	Wed	Thur	Fri
AM					
PM					

From: s.johnson@plab.com
To: m.smith@plab.com
Subject: Meeting Tomorrow

Dear Mark,

I'm writing to confirm the **plan** for tomorrow morning's presentation. It's really important that everything runs smoothly. So, let's start **early** and make sure we don't **waste time**.

Please meet me in the boardroom at a **quarter to** eight. We need to set up the presentation. That will give us plenty of **time** to **spend** practicing it. Then, how about a coffee **break** at **quarter past** nine? The presentation starts at 10 am **sharp**.

Also, the presentation is scheduled to finish at 1 pm. Do you want to have lunch afterwards? Let's **book a table** for **half past** 1. I want to relax after our busy morning!

See you tomorrow,
Sarah

Get ready!

❶ **Before you read the passage, talk about these questions.**

1   What are some phrases used to mark time? How can they be confusing?

2   What are your impressions of people who are early or late to meetings?

Reading

❷ 🎧 **Listen and read this email from one colleague to another. Then, mark the following statements as true (T) or false (F).**

1   __ The woman wants to meet at 7:45 am.

2   __ The presenters will provide coffee.

3   __ The presenters will eat lunch an hour after the meeting.

Vocabulary

❸ **Write a word that is similar in meaning to the underlined part.**

1   The meeting starts at 2 pm <u>exactly</u>.
    _ h _ _ _

2   <u>Make a reservation</u> at the restaurant.
    _ o _ _   _   _ _ _ l _

3   The sales team needs a <u>time to rest</u>.
    _ r _ _ _

4 Match the words (1-7) with the definitions (A-G).

1 __ plan   5 __ quarter to
2 __ early   6 __ quarter past
3 __ waste time   7 __ half past
4 __ spend time

A fifteen minutes before the hour
B to use time to do something
C an arrangement to take place in the future
D thirty minutes after the hour
E before something is scheduled
F to let time go by without doing anything useful
G fifteen minutes after the hour

Listening

5 🎧 **Listen to a conversation between two colleagues. Mark the following statements as true (T) or false (F).**

1 __ The meeting has been cancelled.
2 __ The man plans to practice more.
3 __ The woman suggests eating lunch at 2:15.

6 🎧 **Listen again and complete the conversation.**

Man:	Good morning, Sarah. Ready to go over the presentation?
Woman:	Hi Mark. Actually, there's been a **1** _____ .
Man:	Oh? **2** _____ _____?
Woman:	The meeting is **3** _____ until half past eleven.
Man:	Oh well. We can just spend the extra time **4** _____ .
Woman:	True. And we'll have a longer break. But we're going to miss our lunch reservation.
Man:	I'll call and reschedule.
Woman:	Good idea. Try to **5** _____ a table for a quarter **6** _____ _____ .

Speaking

7 **With a partner, act out the roles below, based on the dialogue from Task 6. Then switch roles.**

USE LANGUAGE SUCH AS:

The meeting is ... until ...
We can spend the extra time ...
Try to ... a table for ...

Student A: Your meeting has been changed. Talk to Student B about:
- new time
- how to spend time
- reservations

Make up a new time for the meeting and lunch.

Student B: Talk with Student A about changes to the schedule.

Writing

8 **Use the conversation from Task 7 to complete your schedule for the day of the meeting. Use expressions about time to schedule the activities. Use tomorrow's date.**

Schedule

Day of the meeting: _____
Practice presentation: _____
Coffee break: _____
Meeting start time: _____
Meeting end time: _____
Lunch: _____

memo

To: All employees
CC: m.weal@klint.com
From: j.davis@klint.com
Subject: Time off policies at KliniTech

Recently, there has been confusion about our time off **policies**. Please review the following.

All employees may take time off when they need it. These **days off** are taken from your paid **vacation time**. We offer 20 days of paid vacation time in addition to public **holidays**. Remember to request time off two weeks **in advance**.

Make arrangements with your supervisor to avoid disrupting work flow. As we are open seven days a week, we cannot have too many employees take time off on **weekends**. Please request **weekdays** off when possible.

Sick time is not to be used for vacation. Notify payroll if time off should come from sick time.

Contact me or my assistant Mary Weal with any questions.

Jillian Davis - Director of Human Resources

holidays

vacation

Get ready!

1 Before you read the passage, talk about these questions.

1 Do you think you should have more or less public holidays in your country?

2 How much vacation time do people get in your country? How does that compare to other countries?

Reading

2 🎧 Listen and read the office memo. Then, choose the correct answers. What is the company's policy towards vacation time?

1 What is the office memo mostly about?
 A rules for taking time off
 B a change in time off policies
 C different ways to request vacation time
 D an addition to the number of paid days off

2 Who do employees speak with to request a day off?
 A their personal supervisor
 B the HR Director's assistant
 C the Human Resources Director
 D the payroll department

3 What can you infer about employees at KliniTech?
 A Most employees ask for time off on weekdays.
 B New employees made mistakes when taking time off.
 C Employees who feel sick are paid when they stay home.
 D Employees must announce vacation plans a week before leaving.

Vocabulary

3 Fill in the blanks with the correct words and phrases from the word bank.

word BANK

policies   time off   vacation time
in advance   day off   weekends

1 Request time off three weeks _____ .

2 Sarah needs a _____ to go to the doctor.

3 Bill dislikes working on _____, but works on Saturday anyway.

4 All companies have _____ for their employees to follow.

5 Only the manager can approve _____ work.

6 Jack's company gives little _____, so he doesn't take long trips.

4 Write a word that is similar in meaning to the underlined part.

1 <u>Pay given to employees who are ill</u> should not be used for vacation. _ _ c _   _ i _ _

2 Did you <u>ask for</u> some time off? _ _ _ u _ s _

3 Petra doesn't have time off for <u>special days of celebration</u>. _ o _ _ _ a _ _

4 The office is only open <u>Monday through Friday</u>. _ _ e _ _ _ _ s

Listening

5 🎧 Listen to a conversation between an employee and his supervisor. Mark the following statements as true (T) or false (F).

1 __ The man is not sure how much vacation time he has.

2 __ The man wants to take a trip to Spain.

3 __ The man already purchased plane tickets.

6 🎧 Listen again and complete the conversation.

Supervisor:	Hi, Jordan. Have a seat. What can I do for you?
Employee:	I want to **1** _____ some time off.
Supervisor:	Sure. Do you know how much **2** _____ _____ you have?
Employee:	Ten days. I **3** _____ _____ _____ on that trip to Spain.
Supervisor:	And **4** _____ do you want leave?
Employee:	Sometime in the first week of June. I **5** _____ _____ to buy plane tickets until I got the time off.
Supervisor:	Well, that sounds fine. Just **6** _____ _____ the request form by Friday.
Employee:	Great, thanks!

Speaking

7 With a partner, act out the roles below, based on the dialogue from Task 6. Then switch roles.

USE LANGUAGE SUCH AS:

What can I do for you?
I want to request some time off.
Please fill out a vacation request form.

Student A: Your employee wants some time off. Ask Student B about:

● vacation time
● dates
● approval

Make up a trip you went on previously.

Student B: Student A is your supervisor. Ask for time off and answer Student A's questions.

Writing

8 Use the conversation from Task 7 to complete the vacation request form.

KliniTech
Vacation Request Form

Name: _____

Amount of Vacation Time: _____

Reason for time off: _____

Dates requested: _____

Supervisor: _____

Approved: Y / N

shipping costs

tax

price quote

Horton's

Horton's is famous for offering high **value** products at excellent prices. Our competitors sell similar items of the same quality for twice as much!

We always deliver great products at a fair price. Our new line of oak furniture, Britannia, is no exception. Our **basic prices** (**excluding tax**), are listed on the back of this brochure. They are very reasonable and we ship anywhere in the world.

Call today to get a free **price quote** that includes all taxes, **fees** and **shipping costs**. Quotes for orders within the USA include **sales tax**, and we can calculate **VAT** for most orders outside the USA.

This new furniture is well **worth** the call!

Get ready!

❶ Before you read the passage, talk about these questions.

1   What are some things that can affect the price of a product?

2   How can you get the best price on a product?

Reading

❷ 🎧 Listen and read part of an advertisement from a furniture retailer. Then, mark the following statements as true (T) or false (F). Say three things you remember from the text.

1   __ Taxes have been added as a part of all listed prices.

2   __ The company lowered the price of its newest line.

3   __ Horton's ships its furniture internationally.

Vocabulary

❸ Match the words (1-7) with the definitions (A-G).

1   __ exclude   5   __ shipping cost

2   __ tax   6   __ sales tax

3   __ fee   7   __ basic price

4   __ worth

A   valuable

B   money that a government collects

C   money that is paid for some service

D   to leave out or not include

E   an extra charge added to purchases that goes to a government

F   the amount a product will cost before additional charges are added

G   the amount of money charged to a customer in order to deliver an item

4 Check (✓) the sentence that uses the underlined parts correctly.

1 __ **A** A <u>good value</u> product is reasonably priced and good quality.

__ **B** Customers pay <u>shipping costs</u> when picking up goods.

2 __ **A** The <u>basic price</u> of this chair includes all taxes and fees.

__ **B** The table cost two hundred dollars before adding <u>VAT</u>.

3 __ **A** Consumers compare <u>price quotes</u> from different shops.

__ **B** The salesman added a <u>sales tax</u> in order to increase his profits.

Listening

5 🎧 Listen to a conversation between a salesman and a customer. Choose the correct answers.

1 What is the dialogue mostly about?

A changing the items in a furniture order

B researching the price of a piece of furniture

C describing price differences in types of furniture

D explaining why a price was higher than expected

2 What is the least expensive charge?

A basic price

B sales tax

C shipping costs

D price quote fee

6 🎧 Listen again and complete the conversation.

Salesman: Horton's Furniture, David speaking. How can I help you?

Customer: Hi. I'd like a free **1** _____ _____ on the oak furniture in your brochure.

Salesman: Yes, the Britannia line. I just **2** _____ _____ _____ what furniture and where you're calling from.

Customer: It's the dining table, and I'm in New York City.

Salesman: Okay. Our **3** _____ _____ is $1,200, but with the **4** _____ _____ it's about $1,300.

Customer: Does that include **5** _____ costs?

Salesman: No. With shipping, it will be another $ **6** _____ .

Customer: Got it, thanks.

Speaking

7 With a partner, act out the roles below, based on the dialogue from Task 6. Then switch roles.

USE LANGUAGE SUCH AS:

How can I help you?

I'm calling about ...

Do you want a price quote?

Student A: You are a salesperson. Tell Student B the price of a product. Include:

● basic price

● price including tax

● any extra fees

Student B: Call Student A about a new product. Ask about the pricing. Make up a piece of furniture you would like to buy.

Writing

8 Use the conversation from Task 7 to complete the sales receipt.

Horton's Sales Receipt

Product: _____

Basic price: _____

Price with tax: _____

Shipping Costs: _____

Delivery to: _____

_____

11 Pay and benefits

salary

rate

Get ready!

1 **Before you read the passage, talk about these questions.**

1 What kinds of jobs pay the highest and lowest salaries?

2 Do you think the most difficult jobs always get the highest wages?

Reading

2 🎧 **Listen and read this pay guide for new employees. Then, choose the correct answers. How can an employee earn more money?**

1 What is the purpose of the guide?

   A to explain the parts of a pay review

   B to describe an available job position

   C to compare salesmen and new employee pay

   D to inform employees of ways to earn more money

2 Employees earn twice as much money by

   A working overtime

   B making commission

   C earning pay raises

   D completing pay reviews

3 What is discussed at a pay review?

   A increasing an employee's work hours

   B an employee's overtime opportunities

   C how well an employee is working

   D an employee's level of commission

Pay Information

All new employees start at **minimum wage**. This means you **earn** $7 per hour from 9am to 5pm. But this is not your entire **salary**. There are many ways to earn more than this.

There is extra pay for evenings and weekends. **Overtime** is 1.5 times the normal **rate**: $10.50 per hour.

We offer a **commission** of 2% on any sales over $50. The commission rises to 3% on sales over $500. Our best sales people can **double** their basic salary with commission!

Every six months there is a **pay review**. In a pay review we sit down together and talk about your **performance**. All employees who perform well get a **raise**. So, show us what you can do!

Vocabulary

3 **Match the words (1-6) with the definitions (A-F).**

1 __ double   4 __ salary

2 __ commission   5 __ minimum wage

3 __ earn   6 __ performance

A to receive something in exchange for work

B a set amount of money an employee will earn per month or year

C the lowest rate of pay that is usually provided to new employees

D a percentage of the profit of a sale given to the employee who arranged the sale

E the act of doing a particular task or job

F to multiply by two

4 Fill in the blanks with the correct words and phrases from the word bank.

word BANK

overtime   rate   raise   pay review

1 Ellen requested to work _____ .
2 Carl has his yearly _____ later today.
3 Keith was happy to earn a _____ .
4 This _____ of pay for this job is too low.

Listening

5 🎧 Listen to a conversation between two employees. Mark the following statements as true (T) or false (F).

1 __ The woman asks for a pay raise.
2 __ The man denies the woman's request.
3 __ The woman can work extra hours on weekends.

6 🎧 Listen again and complete the conversation.

Employee 1:	Hi John. Can you do me a favor?
Employee 2:	Maybe. What is it?
Employee 1:	Well, I'm making **1** _____ _____ . And $7 an hour isn't much.
Employee 2:	Yeah, that's hard. I remember what it was like before my **2** _____ .
Employee 1:	So I'm hoping to earn some **3** _____ . Can I take one of your **4** _____?
Employee 2:	Oh, sorry. I need all the hours I can get. But I know they need help on **5** _____ .
Employee 1:	I didn't know that. How can I **6** _____ _____?
Employee 2:	Just talk to Mary, the weekend manager.

Speaking

7 With a partner, act out the roles below, based on the dialogue from Task 6. Then switch roles.

USE LANGUAGE SUCH AS:

Can you do me a favor?
$7 an hour isn't much.
I need all the hours I can get.

Student A: You want to earn more money. Talk to Student B about:
● current rate of pay
● extra shifts
● overtime

Student B: Answer Student A's questions about increasing pay. Make up a name for the weekend manager.

Writing

8 Make notes about the different ways to increase your salary based on the conversation from Task 7 and the pay guide for employees.

Overtime Hours Request

Name: _____

Current rate of pay: _____

Overtime rate of pay: _____

Reason for Request: _____

_____

_____

When you would like extra hours: _____

25

JOB - compatibility

Thank you for taking our job-compatibility test. Please read your results below.

According to our test, you have a 'conventional' personality type. This means you like to have order in your life. As a result, you work best in organized **environments**. An **office** is a good place for you to work.

The following **occupations** are best suited for conventional personalities:

- **Accountant**   ● **Bank Clerk**   ● **Factory Worker**

But these occupations tend to frustrate conventional personalities:

- **Teacher**   ● **Designer**   ● **Salesperson**

Remember, there's more to a job than how much you earn. Choose an occupation that suits you!

teacher

salesperson

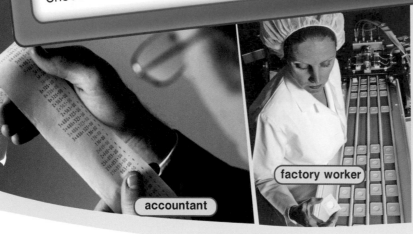
factory worker

accountant

designer

bank clerk

Get ready!

❶ Before you read the passage, talk about these questions.

1   What kind of jobs match your personality? Why?
2   What kind of jobs are not a good match for your personality? Why not?

Reading

❷ 🎧 Listen and read this webpage. Then, mark the following statements as true (T) or false (F). What jobs are best suited for a conventional personality? Why?

1 __ People with conventional personalities have messy offices.
2 __ The person who took the compatibility test should not become a salesperson.
3 __ Teachers frustrate people with conventional personalities.

Vocabulary

❸ Match the words (1-6) with the definitions (A-F).

1 __ accountant   4 __ teacher
2 __ bank clerk   5 __ designer
3 __ factory worker   6 __ salesperson

A   a person who sells products
B   a person who educates others
C   a person who assembles products
D   a person who organizes financial records
E   a person who shapes how something looks
F   a person who works in financial institutions

4 **Place a check (✓) next to the response that answers the question.**

1 Do you consider <u>compatibility</u> an important part of picking a career?

A __ Yes, making enough money matters most.

B __ Yes, feeling comfortable at work is a big deal.

2 Does she want to meet in Mr. Barrett's <u>office</u> later?

A __ Yes, she said to be there at 3:00.

B __ No, I don't want an expensive lunch.

3 Robert needs a quiet <u>environment</u> to study in. Where can he go?

A __ The library is probably the best place.

B __ He is a very good student.

4 What is your father's <u>occupation</u>?

A __ He likes to play chess after work.

B __ He's a salesman at a large store.

Listening

5 🎧 **Listen to a conversation between two friends. Mark the following statements as true (T) or false (F).**

1 __ The woman has a 'conventional' personality type.

2 __ The man thinks that the test results are accurate.

3 __ The woman believes she would be a successful nurse.

6 🎧 **Listen again and complete the conversation.**

Man:	Hey, Jenny. Did you take that **1** _____-_____ test I sent you?
Woman:	Yeah, it was really interesting. The results say I have a **2** '_____' personality.
Man:	Really? What does that mean?
Woman:	It means I'm **3** _____ and helpful.
Man:	So what kind of jobs did it recommend?
Woman:	Any social occupation. Like **4** _____ or teaching.
Man:	I have to **5** _____ . I can see you doing either of those jobs.
Woman:	Thanks. I think I'd make a pretty good **6** _____ .

Speaking

7 **With a partner, act out the roles based on the dialogue from Task 6. Then switch roles.**

USE LANGUAGE SUCH AS:

What is your personality like?

What kind of occupation is right for you?

Student A: You have taken a job-compatibility test. Talk to Student B about:

● personality type

● job recommendations

● your reaction

Choose a personality type. Make up your personal details.

Student B: You sent Student A a job-compatibility test. Talk to Student A about the results.

Writing

8 **Use the conversation from Task 7 and the webpage to complete the job-compatibility test results.**

Job-Compatibility Test Results

You have a _____ personality.

You are _____
_____
_____

You would be compatible with these careers:
_____
_____
_____

You may not be compatible with these careers:
_____
_____
_____

JOB OPENING at TECHWORLD

Full Time: (40 hours per week) We have a full-time position for a computer programmer with 3 or more years of **experience** using C++ programming language. Includes **pension plan**.

Full Time: (45 hours per week) We have vacancies for data-entry clerks. No experience necessary. **Opportunities** for overtime.

Part-Time: (20 hours per week) There are opportunities available for customer service operators on a **permanent** and **temporary** basis. All training will be provided. A **retirement plan** is available for permanent employees.

Techworld employees must sign a **contract** upon employment, and Techworld has the right to **terminate** employees at will.

contract

Get ready!

1 **Before you read the passage, talk about these questions.**

1 When is it better to have a part-time job rather than a full-time job?

2 What are the advantages and disadvantages of temporary work?

Reading

2 🎧 **Listen and read this extract from a job site. Then, mark the following statements as true (T) or false (F). What jobs are on offer?**

1 __ The programming position requires programmers to sign a contract.

2 __ There are multiple positions available for data-entry clerks.

3 __ Temporary employees cannot enroll in a retirement plan.

Vocabulary

3 **Place a check (✓) next to the response that answers the question.**

1 Do you work <u>part-time</u>?

   A __ Yes, I only work on Mondays and Thursdays.

   B __ Yes, I work nine hours a day, five days a week.

2 Do you have <u>experience</u> working with computers?

   A __ Yes, I hope there will be a lot of opportunities.

   B __ Yes, I worked in a computer department.

3 Is your job <u>temporary</u>?

   A __ Yes, it's only for six months.

   B __ Yes, I only work three hours a day.

4 Does your job come with a <u>pension plan</u>?

   A __ Yes, it puts $100 a month into a retirement fund.

   B __ Yes, I am planning to retire at the end of the year.

4 Write a word that is similar in meaning to the underlined part.

A   Tina's job is <u>five days a week, eight hours a day</u>.
    f _ _ _ - _ _ _ e

B   The company has no <u>new jobs available</u>.
    _ a _ _ _ _ _ _ s

C   The company offers a good <u>plan for pensions</u>.
    _ e _ _ _ _ m _ _ _   p _ _ _

D   Everyone has to sign a <u>work agreement</u>.
    _ _ _ t _ _ _ _

E   The boss wants to <u>fire</u> Charles.
    t _ _ m _ _ _ t _

Listening

5 🎧 Listen to a conversation between two employees. Mark the following statements as true (T) or false (F).

1   __ The man is a full-time employee.

2   __ The man has signed up for the retirement plan.

3   __ The woman was first hired as a temporary worker.

6 🎧 Listen again and complete the conversation.

Man:	Excuse me, is this the break room?
Woman:	It is, come in. What's your name?
Man:	Ben. I just started working **1** _____-_____ in customer service.
Woman:	Nice to meet you. I'm Lyn. So how do you like it?
Man:	It's great. I wish I could keep the job **2** _____ and get the **3** _____ _____ .
Woman:	Oh, you're a **4** _____ hire? Don't worry, that's how I started, too.
Man:	But you got a **5** _____ position? How?
Woman:	I told my manager I was **6** _____, and I worked really hard.

Speaking

7 With a partner, act out the roles below, based on the dialogue from Task 6. Then switch roles.

Student A: You are a new employee. Talk to Student B about:

●   your job

●   what you want

●   how Student B achieved a goal

Make up personal details for yourself.

Student B: You are Student A's co-worker. Introduce yourself and answer Student A's questions.

Writing

8 Use the conversation from Task 7 to complete the note from an employee to a manager. Make up a name for the manager.

Dear _____,

This is _____ . I'm writing to inform you that I am interested in _____

I am willing to _____

in order to achieve this goal. Please tell me if there is anything else I can do.

Sincerely, _____

traffic jam

subway

**Commuting Blues?
Try Something new!**

Dawn Lee

Like many people, I **commute** to work by taking **the train**. I used to just stare out the window, but now I make good use of my commute time. And you can, too. It doesn't matter whether you catch **the bus**, train or **subway**. For example, I plan out my work for the morning before reaching my **stop**. Sometimes I **catch up on** my reading. I see other **passengers** knitting or writing to-do lists. The same goes for people in carpools. You'll get work done even while you're stuck in **traffic jams**. It's amazing what you can accomplish before getting to the office!

Get ready!

❶ Before you read the passage, talk about these questions.

1 How far would you be willing to travel every day to go to work?

2 How do most people get to work where you live? Does that system need to be improved?

Reading

❷ 🎧 Listen and read this blog post about commuting to work. Then, mark the following statements as true (T) or false (F). How can someone make the most of his journey to work?

1 __ The author does not drive to work.

2 __ The author believes working in cars is difficult.

3 __ The author often knits on the way to her job.

Vocabulary

❸ Fill in the blanks with the correct words and phrases from the word bank.

word BANK

passenger   accomplishes   catch the bus   stop

1 Jeff _____ a lot on his way to work.
2 Get off the train at the next _____ .
3 The _____ is listening to her MP3 player.
4 Carl should be able to _____ before it leaves.

❹ Read the sentence and choose the correct word.

1 Theresa joined a (**carpool** / **subway**) to save money on gas.
2 Norma was stuck in a bad (**passenger** / **traffic jam**).
3 Daria needs to (**catch up on** / **catch the train**) work.
4 Joseph (**commutes** / **accomplishes**) to work on the subway.

Listening

5 🎧 Listen to a conversation between two commuters riding the train to work. Choose the correct answers.

1 What do the commuters mostly talk about?
   A why they are riding the train
   B the lack of available seating
   C better methods of commuting
   D how long the ride will be

2 What does the woman state is a benefit of riding the train?
   A It is faster than riding the bus.
   B It is less expensive than driving.
   C It is more reliable than a carpool.
   D It avoids waiting in traffic jams.

6 🎧 Listen again and complete the conversation.

Commuter 1:	Excuse me, is anyone sitting here?
Commuter 2:	No, please, **1** _____ a seat.
Commuter 1:	Is it always this crowded? I don't usually **2** _____ _____ _____ .
Commuter 2:	To be honest, I don't know. I'm usually in a carpool with a co-worker.
Commuter 1:	Oh? How did you **3** _____ _____ here, then?
Commuter 2:	She's out sick and I don't have a car. What about you?
Commuter 1:	**4** _____ _____ I catch the bus, but I **5** _____ _____ this morning.
Commuter 2:	Well, at least we won't have to sit in any **6** _____ _____ , right?

Speaking

7 With a partner, act out the roles below, based on the dialogue from Task 6. Then switch roles.

USE LANGUAGE SUCH AS:

Excuse me, is anyone sitting here?
Is it always this crowded?
At least we won't have to …

Student A: You are a commuter on a crowded method of transport. Talk to Student B about:
- available seats
- your usual commute
- Student B's usual commute

Choose a method of transportation.

Student B: You are a commuter on a busy method of transport. Talk to Student A about commuting.

Writing

8 Use the conversation from Task 7 to complete the journal entry. Use today's date.

Date: _____

This morning I_____
so I had to _____
to work instead. But I wasn't the only one!
The train was _____

I also met _____
S/he _____

But it was nice that we didn't _____

carpool

catch the bus

research

applicant

training course

Get ready!

1 **Before you read the passage, talk about these questions.**

1 Should jobs that require special skills pay more than unskilled jobs? Why or why not?

2 Do you think that skilled workers work harder than unskilled workers? Why or why not?

Reading

2 **Read a job advertisement from a newspaper. Then, choose the correct answers.**

1 What is the passage mostly about?

  A the daily tasks of open job positions

  B several vacancies at a research company

  C the need for more skilled workers

  D an opportunity to train workers

2 A research assistant at Bio Labs must

  A be able to enter data.

  B have studied biology.

  C be familiar with computers.

  D be available for day and night shifts.

3 Which of the following is NOT true of maintenance jobs?

  A Training is provided on the job.

  B Applicants must have experience.

  C Some maintenance employees work at night.

  D They require fewer qualifications than research assistants.

Bio Labs seeks both SKILLED and UNSKILLED workers.

Skilled Positions: We need skilled **research** assistants. **Qualifications** required include a degree in biology and research experience in a laboratory setting. Computer skills are **desirable**, but a **training course** is available for new employees.

Unskilled Positions: We also need workers for maintenance positions and basic data entry. Experience is not **necessary** for **applicants** to be considered. These positions have **on the job** training. Maintenance positions are available for both day and evening **shifts**.

To set up an interview, please contact Alice Behan. Call 555-765-9875 between the hours of 9 am and 5 pm, Mondays through Fridays.

Vocabulary

3 **Match the words (1-5) with the definitions (A-E).**

1 __ unskilled   4 __ necessary

2 __ desirable   5 __ on the job

3 __ skilled

A needed

B not requiring special training

C wanted, but not needed

D requiring special training or education

E happening while someone is at work

4 **Write a word that is similar in meaning to the underlined part.**

1 What period of work are you scheduled for?
_ _ _ f _

2 John doesn't meet the requirements.
_ _ _ l _ _ _ _ _ _ _ o _ s

3 Do scientific studies on how the business is performing.
r _ _ _ _ r _ _

4 People trying to get an available job should send their resume to the address below.
a _ _ _ _ _ _ _ _ s

5 An educational class is available.
t _ _ _ n _ _ _   _ _ _ r _ _

5 🎧 **Listen and read to the advert again. Who should you call to arrange an interview?**

Listening

6 🎧 **Listen to a conversation between an applicant and a manager. Mark the following statements as true (T) or false (F).**

1 __ The applicant has experience as a research assistant.

2 __ The applicant doesn't have any lab experience.

3 __ The applicant used computers during lab research for his biology professor.

7 🎧 **Listen again and complete the conversation.**

Manager:	Good morning. Thanks for coming in.
Applicant:	I'm 1 _____ _____ _____ _____ . I'd love to work at Bio Labs.
Manager:	Well, it's a great place to start a career in science. Now, let's talk about your 2 _____ .
Applicant:	Well, I was a 3 _____ assistant in my biology professor's lab.
Manager:	And for how long were you there?
Applicant:	For about two years.
Manager:	Great. So did you 4 _____ his data through 5 _____?
Applicant:	No. He liked to 6 _____ _____ _____ by himself.

Speaking

8 **With a partner, act out the roles below, based on the dialogue from Task 7. Then switch roles.**

USE LANGUAGE SUCH AS:

Thanks for coming in.

It's a great place to start a career in …

And how long were you there?

Student A: You are interviewing an applicant. Ask Student B about:
- experience
- length of experience
- computer use

Student B: You are applying for a job. Answer Student A's questions. Make up your length of experience.

Writing

9 **Use the conversation from Task 8 to complete the manager's notes from the interview. Use your own name.**

Bio Lab Interview Notes

Applicant Name: _____

Position Wanted: _____

Applicant has degree? Y / N

Previous Experience: _____

Length of Experience: _____

Computer Skills: _____

Suggested for hire? Y / N

Glossary

accomplish [V-T-U14] To **accomplish** a task is to complete or do it successfully.

accountant [N-COUNT-U12] An **accountant** is someone whose job is to keep or check financial records.

applicant [N-COUNT-U15] An **applicant** is a person who answers an advertisement for a job vacancy.

appointment [N-COUNT-U7] An **appointment** is a meeting arranged in advance.

approximately [ADV-U6] If someone gives a number **approximately**, the number or amount given is close to the exact amount, but could be a little more or less.

avenue [N-COUNT-U5] An **avenue** is like a street. It's a hard surface where cars and bikes often drive.

avoid [V-T-U3] To **avoid** something means to stay away from it.

bank clerk [N-COUNT-U12] A **bank clerk** is someone who works in a bank and is responsible for general office duties.

basic price [N-COUNT-U10] The **basic price** of a product or service is the price without taxes or fees.

block [N-COUNT-U5] A **block** is a square piece of a city that is built on a grid, such as New York City.

book a table [V- U8] To **book a table** means to reserve a table in a restaurant.

bow [V-I-U1] To **bow** means to bend your waist and lean forward.

break [N-COUNT-U8] A **break** is a time when people stop work for a period of time.

building [N-COUNT-U5] A **building** is a structure such as a house or factory that has walls and a roof.

busy [ADJ-U4] To be **busy** is to have a lot to do, such as work.

calendar [N-COUNT-U7] A **calendar** shows all the days, weeks and months of the year.

carpool [N-COUNT-U14] A **carpool** is a group of people that travel to work together in one car, taking turns driving or sharing the cost of gas.

catch the bus [V PHRASE-U14] Another way to say people go somewhere on a bus is to say that they **catch the bus**.

catch up on [PHRASAL V-U14] To **catch up on** something means to do something which one had intended to do earlier.

cheek [N COUNT-U1] The **cheek** is part of the face. People have two cheeks, one on each side of the mouth.

colleague [N COUNT-U2] A **colleague** is someone with whom a person works.

commission [N-COUNT-U11] A **commission** is a percentage of a sale that a salesman earns as a reward for arranging the sale.

commute [V-I-U14] To **commute** means to travel to and from work.

compatibility [N-UNCOUNT-U12] The **compatibility** of two things is how well they fit together.

contract [N-COUNT-U13] A **contract** is a written agreement that people sign when starting work that states rules and pay.

currency [N-COUNT-U6] **Currency** is the type of money that a country uses.

custom [N COUNT-U1] A **custom** is an action that people traditionally do in a country or region.

day off [N-COUNT-U9] A **day off** is a day when a person does not have to go to work.

deadline [N-COUNT-U7] A **deadline** is the day or time before which something must be completed.

degree [N-COUNT-U15] A **degree** is a title awarded by a university after a person has completed a program of study.

designer [N-COUNT-U12] A **designer** is someone who plans how something will be made, and what it will look like.

desirable [ADJ-U15] If something is **desirable**, then it is wanted but not necessary.

diary [N-COUNT-U7] A **diary** is a book containing spaces for all the days, weeks and months in the year.

discuss [V-T-U3] To **discuss** something means to talk about it in detail.

double [V-T-U11] To **double** something is to increase something to twice its original size or amount.

early [ADV-U8] If something happens **early**, it happens before something else or before it was supposed to.

earn [V-T-U11] To **earn** money is to receive it in exchange for doing work.

enter [V-T-U7] To **enter** something is to put it into something else.

environment [N-COUNT-U12] An **environment** is the situation someone or something lives or works in.

erase [V-T-U7] To **erase** something is to remove it.

estimate [V-T-U6] To **estimate** is to try to give something a value without the number, cost, etc. being exact.

exact [ADJ-U6] If something is **exact**, it is completely correct.

exclude [V-I-U10] To **exclude** something is to leave it out or not to include it.

experience [N-UNCOUNT-U13] **Experience** is work that a person has done in the past.

factory worker [N-COUNT-U12] A **factory worker** is someone who makes things on a production line in a factory.

fee [N-COUNT-U10] A **fee** is an amount of money that is charged for a service.

figures [N-UNCOUNT-U6] **Figures** are numbers that represent amounts, especially official numbers.

firm [ADJ-U1] If something is **firm**, it is tight or not loose.

floor [N-COUNT-U5] A **floor** is one of the levels in a building.

flow [V-I-U3] To **flow** means to continue moving without pause.

forecast [V-T-U6] To **forecast** is to predict what will happen in the future, based on what one knows now.

fraction [N-COUNT-U6] A **fraction** is part of a whole number, such as 1/2.

full-time [ADJ/ADV-U13] **Full-time** work is working forty hours a week or more.

get back [V-T-U4] To **get back** to something is to return to it.

greet [V-T-U1] To **greet** someone means to say hello to him or her.

half past [N-UNCOUNT-U8] **Half past** an hour means thirty minutes past the hour.

have time [V PHRASE-U4] When people **have time**, they are not busy and can spend time doing something or helping someone.

holiday [N-COUNT-U9] A **holiday** is a special day that everyone in a region celebrates.

hurt feelings [V-I-U4] When a person **hurts someone's feelings**, they make that person feel unhappy.

I'd like you to meet … [PHRASE-U2] **I'd like you to meet …** is used to introduce one person to another.

in advance [ADV-U9] To do something **in advance** is to do it before it needs to be done.

Glossary

in common [ADJ-U2] If two people have something **in common**, they are similar in some way.

instructions [N-COUNT-U5] **Instructions** are information that tell you how to do or use something.

introduce [V-T-U2] To **introduce** someone means to help that person meet someone else by telling both people each other's names and other basic information.

involve [V-T-U3] To **involve** something means to include it. If your job involves typing, it means you type as part of your job.

It was nice meeting you [PHRASE-U1] **It was nice meeting you** is used to say goodbye to someone for the first time in a formal situation.

journey [N-COUNT-U5] A **journey** is the time spent to go from one place to another, especially a long distance.

kiss [V-I or T-U1] To **kiss** means to touch someone or something with the lips.

left out [ADJ-U2] If someone feels **left out**, that person feels lonely because nobody is talking to him or her.

Let me introduce you to … [PHRASE-U2] **Let me introduce you to …** is used to introduce one person to another.

living [N COUNT-U3] A **living** is what someone does in order to earn money.

main entrance [N-COUNT-U5] The **main entrance** of a building is the main door that you use to enter a building.

marital status [N UNCOUNT-U3] **Marital status** is a person's status as single, married or divorced.

mention [V-T-U2] To **mention** something means to talk about it for a short time.

necessary [ADJ-U15] If something is **necessary**, then it is needed.

occupation [N COUNT-U2 & U12] An **occupation** is your/a job.

office [N-COUNT-U12] An **office** is a room or building where people work. Typically, each will have their own desk and computer.

on the job [ADJ-U15] If something happens **on the job**, it occurs while someone is at work.

opportunity [N-COUNT-U13] An **opportunity** is a chance to do something.

overtime [N-UNCOUNT-U11] **Overtime** is work done at a job beyond the agreed upon number of hours. Overtime work pays more than the usual rate of pay.

overtime [N-UNCOUNT-U13] **Overtime** is the work done over the agreed number of hours on a contract.

part-time [ADJ/ADV-U13] **Part-time** work is less than 40 hours a week.

passenger [N-COUNT-U14] A **passenger** is a person who travels in a vehicle such as a bus or train but does not drive it.

pay [N-UNCOUNT-U11] **Pay** is the amount of money people receive from their employers for working.

pension [N-COUNT-U13] A **pension** is the money a person collects from a former employer after retiring.

pension plan [N-COUNT-U13] A **pension plan** is a system in which an employer puts an employee's money into a fund that the employee can use after retiring.

percent [N-COUNT-U6] A **percent** is a part out of a total 100 parts, like 50%.

percentage [N-COUNT-U6] A **percentage** is an amount that is expressed as part of a 100.

perform [V-I-U11] To **perform** means to do something.

performance [N-UNCOUNT-U11] **Performance** is the act of doing something.

permanent [ADJ-U13] A **permanent** job does not have a specific end date.

phrase [N-COUNT-U4] A **phrase** is a few words or a short sentence.

plan [N-COUNT-U8] A **plan** is an arrangement for what is going to happen.

Pleased to meet you [PHRASE-U1] **Pleased to meet you** is used when meeting someone for the first time in a formal situation.

policy [N-COUNT-U9] A **policy** is method of action to guide future decisions.

polite [ADJ-U1] If people are **polite**, they show they respect to other people.

price quote [N-COUNT-U10] A **price quote** is a statement of how much a product will cost with all taxes and fees.

priority [N-COUNT-U7] A **priority** is something that is very important and must be done before all other things.

qualification [N-COUNT-U15] A **qualification** is a requirement that someone must meet in order to be eligible for a job.

quarter [N-COUNT-U6] A **quarter**, in business terms, is a period of three months.

quarter past [N-UNCOUNT-U8] **Quarter past** an hour means fifteen minutes after the hour.

quarter to [N-UNCOUNT-U8] **Quarter to** an hour means fifteen minutes before the hour.

raise [N-COUNT-U11] A **raise** is an increase in pay, usually given after an employee has excelled or done well.

rate [N-COUNT-U11] A **rate** is the amount of something that changes over a given period of time.

relationship [N COUNT-U2] A **relationship** is the way in which a person knows and interacts with another person.

religion [N COUNT-U3] A **religion** is a belief in a god or gods.

request [V-T-U9] To **request** something is to ask for it.

research [N-UNCOUNT-U15] **Research** is serious and in-depth study.

retirement [N-UNCOUNT-U13] **Retirement** is the stage of life in which a person stops working.

retirement plan [N-COUNT-U13] A **retirement plan** is a plan in which an employer puts money into a fund that the employee can use after retiring.

review [N-COUNT-U11] A **review** is a process in which something is looked at in order to decide how well it has been done.

right [N-UNCOUNT-U5] **Right** is the direction that is on the right-side of your body. It is the opposite of left.

rude [ADJ-U4] Someone is **rude** when he or she is very unfriendly.

run [V-U4] To **run** is to hurry and go somewhere or begin doing something.

salary [N-COUNT-U11] A **salary** is the fixed amount of money you receive regularly from your employer.

sales tax [N-UNCOUNT-U10] **Sales tax** is the additional money that an authority collects on goods or services.

salesperson [N-COUNT-U12] A **salesperson** is someone who persuades customers to buy a product.

schedule [N-COUNT-U7] A **schedule** is a plan that gives events and the times they will happen.

schedule [V-U7 & U8+950+2] To **schedule** is to arrange an event or activity for a particular time.

shake hands [V PHRASE-U1] To **shake hands** means to hold someone's hand with your hand and lift it up and down.

sharp [ADV-U8] If an event starts at 10 am **sharp**, it starts exactly at that time.

shift [N-COUNT-U15] A **shift** is a period of time that a person is scheduled to work.

shipping costs [N-UCOUNT-U10] **Shipping costs** are the additional payments that are made to have a product delivered.

sick time [N-UNCOUNT-U9] **Sick time** is pay that is given to employees who are sick and cannot come to work.

skilled [ADJ-U15] If a worker is **skilled**, he or she has been trained or educated to do a specific type of job.

small talk [N UNCOUNT-U3] **Small talk** is polite conversation with someone that a person doesn't know well.

spend time [V-U8] To **spend time** is to use time doing something.

steer a conversation [V-I or T-U1] To **steer a conversation** means to direct a conversation towards or away from a particular topic.

stop [N-COUNT-U14] A **stop** is a location where a vehicle lets passengers on and off, such as a station or bus-stop.

subway [N-COUNT-U14] The **subway** is an underground train found in many large cities.

take the train [V-T-U14] Someone who goes by train can also be said to **take the train**.

take up time [V PHRASEU4] To **take up time** is to use a lot of time.

tax [N-COUNT-U10] A **tax** is an amount of money that is paid to an authority for public purposes.

teacher [N-COUNT-U12] A **teacher** is someone who educates other people.

temporary [ADJ-U13] A **temporary** job is one that has a specific end date and usually only lasts a few months.

terminate [V-T-U13] To **terminate** an employee is to end that person's employment immediately.

-th [SUFFIX-U5] **-th** is added to the end of ordinal numbers, as in fourth, fifth, and sixth, which show the order of something.

time off [N-UNCOUNT-U9] **Time off** is an amount of time that people do not have to work.

tone [N-UNCOUNT-U4] **Tone** is the sound of one's voice, such as a polite or angry tone.

topic [N COUNT-U3] A **topic** is a subject that people talk about or study.

traffic jam [N-COUNT-U14] A **traffic jam** is an event in which the cars on a busy road are stopped because there is an accident or too many cars on the road.

training course [N-COUNT-U15] A **training course** is a class that teaches people a new skill to prepare them for a job.

unfortunately [ADV-U4] **Unfortunately** is used to introduce something negative or that one wishes wasn't true.

unskilled [ADJ-U15] If a worker is **unskilled**, he or she has not been trained or educated to do a specific type of job.

up-to-date [ADJ-U7] When something is **up-to-date**, it contains the latest information or changes.

vacancy [N-COUNT-U13] A **vacancy** is an available position.

vacation time [N-UNCOUNT-U9] **Vacation time** is the time that people do not have to work but are still paid.

value [N-UNCOUNT-U10] The **value** of something is the worth or importance that it has.

VAT [N-UNCOUNT-U10] **VAT** or value added tax is the name for a national sales tax in many countries.

waste time [V-U8] To **waste time** is to allow time to go by without doing anything useful.

weather [N UNCOUNT-U3] The **weather** is the temperature, rain and wind etc.

weekday [N-COUNT-U9] **Weekdays** are Monday, Tuesday, Wednesday, Thursday and Friday.

weekend [N-COUNT-U9] The **weekend** is usually Saturday and Sunday.

worth [ADJ-U10] If something is **worth** a lot, it's value in money is high.

Career Paths

Business English

Book 2

John Taylor
Jeff Zeter

Express Publishing

Table of Contents

Omega Electronics COMES OUT with NEW Galaxy

Two years ago, Omega **launched** the Omega Star mobile phone. Now, our designers have **developed** an even better phone. We are pleased to announce the arrival of the Omega Galaxy. The Galaxy is **manufactured** solely for use by TeleCom Wireless customers. Omega is proud to partner with the nation's leading mobile service provider.

The Galaxy comes with all the amazing **features** that the Star does. But it has a longer battery life and brighter display screen. It has been **assembled** to Omega's **quality** standards. **Benefits** of the Galaxy include a more user-friendly touch screen and higher speed Internet capabilities. For customers who prefer a simpler phone, the Star will remain available for purchase.

The Galaxy will be **shipped from** our factories this week. Then, they will be **distributed by** TeleCom Wireless to their stores across the country. The phone will be available for purchase in TeleCom stores on May 13.

Get ready!

1 Before you read the passage, talk about these questions.

1 What are some things people look for when purchasing a product?
2 What kinds of advertisements are the most successful? Why?

Reading

2 🎧 **Listen and read the press release from a mobile phone store. Then, mark the following statements as true (T) or false (F). How is the Galaxy phone better than the star phone?**

1 ___ The Star model mobile phone is no longer for sale.
2 ___ The Galaxy will work with only one service provider.
3 ___ The Galaxy is available directly from Omega Electronics.

Vocabulary

3 **Match the words (1-7) with the definitions (A-G).**

1 ___ features   5 ___ assemble
2 ___ launch   6 ___ benefit
3 ___ develop   7 ___ manufacture
4 ___ ship from

A to send or mail a product from a specific location
B to design or build something new
C to begin selling a new product
D the special things that an item has or can do
E to put pieces of something together
F to create something using machinery
G the good or helpful qualities of something

4 Write a word that is similar in meaning to the underlined part.

1 The phone is <u>given or sold</u> by only one company.
d _ _ t _ _ b u _ _ _   _ y

2 Has the new phone <u>become available for sale</u>?
_ o m _   o _ _

3 This MP3 player is of <u>the highest standard</u> construction.
_ _ a _ i t _

Listening

5 🎧 **Listen to a conversation between two employees. Check (✓) the items that will be changed in the press release.**

1 ❏ price   4 ❏ features
2 ❏ shipping date 5 ❏ assembly
3 ❏ distribution   6 ❏ quality standards

6 🎧 **Listen again and complete the conversation.**

Employee 1:	Well, 1 _____ _____ _____ with the Galaxy press release.
Employee 2:	Oh? What's wrong?
Employee 1:	I guess there's a change in the 2 _____ _____ .
Employee 2:	So it won't be 3 _____ on time?
Employee 1:	No, definitely not. Everything has been pushed back two weeks.
Employee 2:	Okay, I'll make the changes to those items right away. Anything else?
Employee 1:	Well, we want to keep customers interested, even though there's a delay. So we want to add some more detail to the 4 _____ _____ section.
Employee 2:	Will do. What's the cause for the delay, anyway?
Employee 1:	The phones were being 5 _____ too quickly. They weren't meeting 6 _____ _____ .

Speaking

7 **With a partner, act out the roles below, based on the dialogue from Task 6. Then switch roles.**

USE LANGUAGE SUCH AS:

Do you have a moment?
There's a change in the …
Everything has been pushed back two weeks.

Student A: A press release must be changed. Talk to Student B about:
● what must change
● what to add
● cause of changes
Make up a cause for the changes.

Student B: Talk to Student A to find out what to change on a press release.

Writing

8 **You are writing a new press release for a product launch. Use the conversation from Task 7 and the press release to update a press release for a new mobile phone. Talk about:**

● product description
● new dates
● extra features

_____
_____
_____
_____

Sneakers DiRect

●○○

Online or **in our stores:**

The **BEST** sneakers for your feet and your wallet.

Today's Online Specials

Today Only: Our #1 selling sneakers at **wholesale** price!

Click here for details.

Selected styles: Buy one get one at half price!

Click here to view styles.

Free **shipping** on all orders over $75.00

Shop our catalogue

Mail Order:
14 Factory Rd
Del Mar, DE 98509

Phone Order:
1-800-999-5555

Open Monday–Saturday
9AM to 6PM

*Include **item number** with your order.

Sneakers Direct is a leader in **e-commerce**. Check our website daily for exclusive offers.

We **promise** that our footwear is the best quality at the best price. Return your items free of charge if you are not completely satisfied.

Our prices are guaranteed! If you find a lower price, we'll **match** it!

item number

Tired of **retailers**? Call toll-free to ask about **direct sales**.

Get ready!

❶ Before you read the passage, talk about these questions.

1 Do you prefer to shop online or in person? Why?

2 What are the risks of shopping online?

Reading

❷ 🎧 Listen and read the web page for a shoe store. Then, mark the following statements as T (true) or F (false).

1 __ Customers will pay shipping for a $50.00 order.

2 __ The company will reduce prices lower than any competitor.

3 __ Direct sales can be arranged on the website.

Vocabulary

❸ Choose the word that is closest in meaning to the underlined part.

1 Here is the new magazine with photos and descriptions of products for sale.

A direct sales   B e-commerce   C catalogue

2 The salesman guaranteed that the shoes were comfortable.

A promised   B matched   C retailed

3 The cost to mail products added $10.00.

A item number   B shipping   C offer

4 Online business is important to most retailers.

A mail order   B catalogue   C e-commerce

5 Change to the level of the price our competitors offer.

A promise   B sell   C match

4 Read the sentence pairs. Choose where the words best fit in the blanks.

1 **mail order / item number**

Write the _____ on the form.

Complete this form to place a _____ .

2 **retailers / wholesale**

_____ prices are usually very low.

GrantCo is one of the country's biggest _____ .

3 **direct sales / phone order**

Call this number to place a _____ .

Locate a _____ location nearby.

Listening

5 🎧 Listen to a conversation between a telephone sales representative and a customer. Mark the following statements as true (T) or false (F).

1 ___ The customer lost the item number.

2 ___ The sneakers are not available in the requested color.

3 ___ The total cost is $64.

6 🎧 Listen again and complete the conversation.

Representative:	Thank you for calling Sneakers Direct. 1 _____ _____ _____ _____ you today?
Customer:	I'd like to order some shoes from your catalogue, please.
Representative:	Great. Do you have the 2 _____ _____?
Customer:	Yes. It's GH1184.
Representative:	The 3 _____ _____ Sneakers?
Customer:	Yes. In a size 11, please.
Representative:	We do have those shoes available in your size. What 4 _____ _____ _____ like?
Customer:	Do you have them in green?
Representative:	Yes. The 5 _____ is $55.00 plus $9.00 shipping.

0123 5420 21454

Speaking

7 With a partner, act out the roles below, based on the dialogue from Task 6. Then switch roles.

USE LANGUAGE SUCH AS:

I'd like to order some …

What color would you like?

And if I decide I don't like them?

Student A: You are a customer who wants to order sneakers. Talk to Student B about:

● shoes

● color

● guarantees

Make up a size and color you want.

Student B: You are a sales representative. Answer Student A's questions.

Writing

8 You are writing a page in a catalogue for a company. Use the conversation from Task 7 and the web page to write a description of a type sneakers available for sale. Talk about:

● What sizes are available

● What colors are available

● What the company's return policy is

_____

_____

_____

_____

_____

7

receipt

satisfied

model number

refund

ELECTRONICS ⊦-WW-⊦ NATION
S E R V I C E   D E P A R T M E N T **Manual**

When a customer enters the **service department** he or she should always be greeted with a smile. Every product sold at Electronics Nation comes with our famous **guarantee**. We offer a **refund** or **replacement** for a full year if the customer is not **satisfied** for any reason. However, there are a few things you will need from the customer:

First, we need the original **receipt** or a copy of the **warranty**. One of these documents is required to process the **return**.

Next, we need the **make** and **model number** of the item they wish to return.

Finally, we need a brief written explanation on the return form.

If the customer would like to replace the item, send him out to the showroom. If he would prefer a refund, send him to the business office with the completed return form.

| Chapter 4 | Product Returns |

Get ready!

❶ Before you read the passage, talk about these questions.

1 When was the last time you returned a product? Why did you do it?

2 What are some ways companies compensate people who return products?

Reading

❷ 🎧 Listen and read the page from a customer service manual. Then, choose the correct answers. What should customers give the service department?

1 What is NOT required to return an item?

    A a completed form

    B a record of the item's purchase

    C an identification number for the type of item

    D a description of the item's condition

2 Electronics Nation offers

    A free repairs on all purchases.

    B to replace unsatisfactory purchases.

    C a refund within two years of a purchase.

    D returns without a receipt or a copy of the warranty.

3 Employees must note the ___ of returns.

    A repair cost

    B time of purchase

    C color and style

    D make and model number

Vocabulary

❸ Match the words (1-5) with the definitions (A-E).

1 ___ make   4 ___ guarantee

2 ___ satisfied   5 ___ service department

3 ___ receipt

A the printed record of a sale

B the name that identifies who produced the product

C the place where consumers can receive help

D being happy with one's purchase

E an assurance

4 Fill in the blanks with the correct words and phrases from the word bank.

word BANK

customer service   refunds   replacement
warranty   model number

1 Good _____ keeps customers coming back.

2 If a product is broken, customers may get a _____ .

3 The make and _____ of the stereo is printed on the box.

4 The returns department also gives _____ .

5 Do you have a copy of the _____?

Listening

5 🎧 **Listen to a conversation between a customer service representative and a customer. Mark the statements as true (T) or false (F).**

1 __ The man did not bring the original receipt.

2 __ The stereo did not work.

3 __ The man will receive a refund.

6 🎧 **Listen again and complete the conversation.**

Representative:	Okay. I'll need to see the **1** _____ _____, please.
Customer:	Oh. I don't have it anymore. I brought the **2** _____, though. Here you go.
Representative:	That'll work, thanks. Do you know **3** _____ _____ the stereo is?
Customer:	It's the Sonic 200.
Representative:	Let's see … and the model number is here on the warranty. Now, why are you **4** _____ the stereo?
Customer:	I don't really like the sound quality. It just wasn't **5** _____ _____ _____ .
Representative:	Okay. Now, we can only **6** _____ _____ if you have the receipt.
Customer:	But I can get a **7** _____, right?

Speaking

7 **With a partner, act out the roles below, based on the dialogue from Task 6. Then switch roles.**

USE LANGUAGE SUCH AS:

I'd like to return this stereo.

I'll need to see the …

Pick something out in the showroom.

Student A: You are a customer service representative. Student B wants to return a product. Talk to Student B about:

● receipt

● reason for return

● refunds and replacements

Make up a model number for the product.

Student B: You are returning a product. Answer Student A's questions.

Writing

8 **You are a customer service representative processing a return. Use the conversation from Task 7 to fill out a return form. Talk about:**

● The make and model number of the item

● Whether the customer has the receipt

● Why the customer was not satisfied with the purchase

_____

_____

_____

_____

_____

Business Blog Weekly

Good etiquette on the telephone can make or break your relationship with a client. **Courtesy** should start with the person who answers the telephone. Always begin by identifying yourself. Say something like, **"Hello, this is..."** Give the person as much information as you can. Tell them the name of your company, **"I'm calling from..."**

Ask for the person you wish to speak with by name, using phrases like, **"Could I speak to...?"** or **"May I speak to...?"** Or ask, **"Is...available?"**

At some companies, with busy **switchboards**, it is better to simply ask, **"Can you connect me to extension..."**

Remember, ending the call on a polite note is important too. Say something like, **"Nice speaking to you,"** or **"Thank you for your time."** Follow up with **"I will call you back on..."** And remember to do it.

switchboard

Get ready!

❶ Before you read the passage, talk about these questions.

1 How do you answer phone calls from friends? From business partners?

2 Why is having good phone etiquette important in business?

Reading

❷ 🎧 Listen and read the post from a business blog. Then, read the paraphrase of the article. Fill in the blanks with the correct words and phrases from the word bank. Explain what good phone etiquette is.

 **BANK**

**by name   connected   telephone
extension   courtesy**

It is important for businesspeople to have good **1**_____ etiquette. **2**_____ should be used whenever speaking to anyone on the phone. Callers should identify themselves and then ask to speak to someone **3**_____ . They can also ask to be **4**_____ to a(n) **5**_____ . A good way to end a call is to thank the person they're speaking to for his or her time.

Vocabulary

❸ Place the words and phrases from the word bank under the correct heading.

 **BANK**

**thank you for your time   Hello this is ...
Is ... available   Nice speaking with you
Could I speak to ...**

Greeting	Ending	Asking for someone
_____	_____	_____
	_____	_____

4 Write a word or phrase that is similar in meaning to the underlined part.

1 Hello, my name is Robert and <u>I work for</u> Bronson Industries.
   I'_ _ _ a _ _ in _   f _ _ _

2 <u>I would like to talk to</u> the director of the sales department.
   _ ay _ s _ _ a _ _ o

3 Please <u>expect a call from me</u> on Thursday.
   I _ _ ll _ a _ _ y _ _ _ a c _

4 It is important to behave with <u>politeness</u> on the telephone.
   _ o u _ _ _ s _

5 Will you <u>direct my phone call to</u> Number 443?
   C _ _ _ o _ _ _ n n _ _ t _ e _ _ e x _ _ s _ o n

Listening

5 🎧 **Listen to a telephone conversation between a receptionist and a sales representative. Mark the following statements as true (T) or false (F).**

1 __ The man is calling to place an order.

2 __ The receptionist offers two ways to leave a message.

3 __ The man asks if he can call Ms. Jones at home.

6 🎧 **Listen again and complete the conversation.**

Sales Rep:	**1** _____ _____ _____ to Susie Jones, please?
Receptionist:	I'm sorry, Susie isn't in right now. I would be happy to take a message for you.
Sales Rep:	Well, it's a rather **2** _____ _____ to an order that I should discuss with her. Is there a better time to reach her?
Receptionist:	She'll be out until tomorrow, unfortunately.
Sales Rep:	Oh, okay. I'd better leave a message with you, then.
Receptionist:	Well, I could also **3** _____ _____ _____ her voicemail. She might check that before she comes into the office.
Sales Rep:	Oh good, that would be wonderful.
Receptionist:	Okay. I'm connecting you now. **4** _____ _____ _____ _____, Mr. Peters.
Sales Rep:	And you, too. **5** _____ _____ _____ _____ .

Speaking

7 With a partner, act out the roles below, based on the dialogue from Task 6. Then switch roles.

USE LANGUAGE SUCH AS:

Good morning ...This is ... speaking.

I'm sorry. ... isn't in right now.

I'd better leave a message with you.

Student A: You are calling a business client. Talk to Student B about:

● speaking to your client
● messages
● your thanks

Make up a name for you client.

Student B: You are a receptionist. Student A calls to speak to a client who is not in. Answer Student A's questions. Make up a name for your caller.

Writing

8 You are a receptionist. Use the conversation from Task 7 to leave a note for a client who missed a call. Talk about:

● Who called
● What he or she called about
● What options you provided him or her with
● How the caller reacted

_____

_____

_____

_____

Email for Beginners: A quick lesson

Let's begin with **email addresses**. These are made up of three parts:

- The person's name, nickname, etc. (for example: bill, bill_williams, bwilliams)
- The @ **symbol** (this means "at")
- The web address where the account is located (for example: SupplyStore.com, cyberlink.net)

So a complete address might look like this: bwilliams@cyberlink.net.

On your email program, you'll see places to enter the address your **message** is going to, the address it is from and the **subject** of the message. Above, or sometimes below, this on the page, you will see a button that allows you to include an **attachment**.

When you receive a message, you have several options:

- Save or **delete** it
- Reply to the sender or **reply to all**
- **Forward** it to someone else

A note on **formal vs. informal style**:

Emails are generally informal. Still, good business etiquette dictates that business **correspondence** should be more formal.

Get ready!

① Before you read the passage, talk about these questions.

1 How can email be useful in business?
2 What problems can be caused by email?

Reading

② 🎧 Listen and read the tutorial on email. Then, use the completed table to present emails to the class. Complete the table using information from the tutorial.

Parts of an email address	
Options after receiving a message	

Vocabulary

③ Match the words (1-5) with the definitions (A-E).

1 __ message
2 __ attachment
3 __ subject
4 __ formal
5 __ informal

A being serious and official
B the main part of an email
C being relaxed and casual
D a file that is sent along with an email
E the title of an email

4 Check (✓) the sentence that uses the underlined part correctly.

1 __ **A** Mary's <u>email address</u> is mbrown@bluesky.com.

__ **B** If you <u>forward</u> an email it goes to the trash box.

2 __ **A** Click <u>reply to all</u> so that only Jay sees the response.

__ **B** Delete old messages <u>from the inbox</u>.

3 __ **A** <u>Names come before</u> the @ symbol in most email addresses.

__ **B** An <u>option</u> indicates what the email is about.

Listening

5 🎧 **Listen to a conversation between two co-workers. Choose the correct answers.**

1 What is the conversation mostly about?

A the details of the finance report

B how to create a new email address

C why the man did not receive an email

D a mistake the man made on a report

2 What information does the man provide?

A his new email address

B how to forward an email

C the name of an attachment

D which employee he sent the report to

6 🎧 **Listen again and complete the conversation.**

Employee 2: That's 1 _____ . I didn't get an email from you today.

Employee 1: I'm sure it went out, since I also sent it to Michelle Richards. She opened it this morning.

Employee 2: Maybe Michelle can just 2 _____ _____ _____ _____ .

Employee 1: I'd rather 3 _____ _____ why it didn't arrive.

Employee 2: Well, what address did you send it to?

Employee 1: Let's see. It was BillStephenson@cranstonindustries.com.

Employee 2: Oh, that's it. That's my old 4 _____ _____ .

Employee 1: I didn't know it had changed. 5 _____ _____ _____ _____ ?

Employee 2: It's just B.Stephenson@cranstonindustries 6 _____ .

Speaking

7 **With a partner, act out the roles below, based on the dialogue from Task 6. Then switch roles.**

USE LANGUAGE SUCH AS:

Did you get that …

I didn't get an email from you today …

What address did you send it to?

Student A: You sent an important file to Student B. Talk about:

● receiving the file

● investigating the problem

● finding a solution

Make up the name of someone you sent it to.

Student B: Student A tried to send you an email. Talk about:

● receiving the file

● possible solutions

● email address changes

Writing

8 **You are a manager and there has been a problem sending email to an employee. Use the conversation from Task 7 and the email tutorial to write an email to all employees that explains the problem and how to avoid it in the future. Talk about:**

● The cause of the problem

● How it was solved

● What employees must do to avoid the problem

_____

_____

_____

_____

_____

_____

Get ready!

1 Before you read the passage, talk about these questions.

1 When is a letter an appropriate method of communication? When is it not?

2 In what ways do business letters differ from personal letters?

Dear...
greeting

I look forward to hearing from you.
closing

Yours truly,
ending

Business Letters 10.1

A Guide for the Modern Professional

As a professional, you must have the skills to write a clear and polite business letter. The example below will show you the elements of a good letter.

Sender's full name
Return Address

Today's date
Recipient's full name
Recipient's Address
Salutation or **Greeting** ("Dear Ms. Smith"),
Your reason for writing and the other information goes here.
Closing ("Thank you for your time." "I look **forward** to hearing from you." etc.)
Ending ("Sincerely," "Yours truly," etc.)
Sender's **signature**
Sender's typed name
Enclosures:

After "Enclosures," list any documents that you are sending along with the letter. This includes photographs, forms to be returned, receipts, etc.

Follow this simple guide, and you will be writing perfect business letters in no time.

Reading

2 🎧 **Listen and read the excerpt from a manual. Then, mark the following statements as true (T) or false (F). What did you learn from the text?**

1 __ Business letters never include a recipient's first name.

2 __ A signature is typed at the bottom of the letter.

3 __ List any attached documents as enclosures.

Vocabulary

3 Read the sentence pairs. Choose where the words best fit in the blanks.

1 sender / recipient

The _____ types the letter and puts it in the mail.

When it arrives at its destination, it is opened by the _____ .

2 closing / signature

A person's _____ is handwritten beneath the closing.

It is a good idea to thank the reader in the _____ .

3 greeting / full name

The _____ should begin with, "Dear Mr. or Ms."

Write your _____ , not just your first or last.

4 **Choose the word that is closest in meaning to the underlined part.**

1 Make sure to note any <u>enclosures</u>.

  A closing   B items to be sent later

  C items included here

2 Choose a suitable <u>ending</u> for your letter.

  A closing   B hello   C sign

3 Use the correct <u>salutation</u> in your letter.

  A greeting   B ending   C remarks

4 Don't forget to include the <u>return address</u>.

  A email address   B recipient's address

  C sender's address

Listening

5 🎧 **Listen to a conversation between an office manager and her new assistant. Mark the following statements as true (T) or false (F).**

1 __ The letter is intended to sign up a new client.

2 __ The letter will list a form as an enclosure.

3 __ The letter will include an envelope for a reply.

6 🎧 **Listen again and complete the conversation.**

Assistant:	Okay. And is there a particular **1** _____ you use with him?
Manager:	Oh, just "Dear Mr. Smith" is fine.
Assistant:	Got it. And what's the reason for writing to Mr. Smith?
Manager:	He just opened a second office, so we need to **2** _____ _____ _____ _____ .
Assistant:	Should I include the update form with the letter?
Manager:	Yes, please. And **3** _____ _____ _____ _____ _____ so he knows to look for it.
Assistant:	I'll print an envelope with our **4** _____ _____ and include that, too.
Manager:	Good thinking. Please bring it to me when you have finished so I can add my **5** _____ .
Assistant:	I'll have it ready in just a minute.

Speaking

7 **With a partner, act out the roles below, based on the dialogue from Task 6. Then switch roles.**

USE LANGUAGE SUCH AS:

Could you type …?

Should I include …

Please bring it to me for my signature …

Student A: You need Student B to type a letter for you. Talk to Student B about:

- recipient
- purpose
- enclosures

Make up a name for the recipient.

Student B: You are Student A's assistant. Talk to Student A about the letter.

Writing

8 **You are an assistant. Use the conversation from Task 7 and the excerpt from the manual to write a business letter to a client. Use today's date. Make up a name for the sender. Include:**

- The recipient's full name
- A greeting
- The purpose of the letter
- Any enclosures

_____

_____

_____

_____

_____

_____

7 Faxes

Get ready!

1 **Before you read the passage, talk about these questions.**

1 How can a fax machine save businesses time and money?

2 Do you think the fax machine will be replaced by online technology? Why or why not?

fax number

document

send a fax

insert

How to Send a Fax

Make sure that your pages reach the right person. Follow these steps and your **documents** will be on their way.

Our **fax number**: (333) 555-2111

*Always include a **cover sheet** with the following information:

- Your name
- Your company's name
- Your telephone number
- The name of the person you are sending the fax to
- The date
- The number of pages
- The **subject**

***Insert** the pages into the fax machine, printed side down.

*Enter the fax number you want to send to using the **keypad**.

*The pages will be scanned by the machine.

*The machine will give you a **confirmation** if the pages have **gone through** properly. If the fax does not go through, you will need to **resend**.

*First, telephone the other person and tell them that you are trying to **fax something over**.

*Repeat the earlier steps and wait for confirmation.

Reading

2 🎧 **Listen and read the poster telling how to send a fax. Then, read the summary of the passage. Fill in the blanks with the correct words and phrases from the word bank. Tell the class how to send a fax.**

WOrd BANK

resend   cover sheet   go through
send a fax   **confirmation**

The manual gives instructions about how to
1_____ . It lists the information to include on
the **2** _____ . The sender is instructed to wait
to see whether the fax will **3** _____ properly.
If not, the sender should telephone the recipient.
Next, he or she should try to **4** _____ it and
wait for **5** _____ that it has worked.

Vocabulary

3 **Write a word that is similar in meaning to the underlined part.**

1 Use the <u>number buttons on the fax machine</u>.
k _ _ p _ _

2 Did the machine give a <u>notification that the document was sent</u>?
_ o n _ _ _ _ a t _ _ _

3 The telephone number goes on the <u>first page of the fax</u>.
c _ _ e r _ h e _ _

4 Please <u>send this through the fax machine</u>.
_ e n _ _ f _ _

5 Type the <u>code for the recipient's fax machine</u>.
_ _ x n _ _ b _ _

4 Place a check (✓) next to the response that answers the question.

1 Did Ms. Chen fax something over to the client?

    A __ Yes, but it did not go through.

    B __ Yes, we need to try to send it again.

2 Do I need to resend the fax?

    A __ Yes, you should try it again.

    B __ She doesn't need to know.

3 What is the subject of the fax?

    A __ The fax number is right here.

    B __ It's about the upcoming merger.

4 Should the pages be inserted face down?

    A __ No, I did not receive a confirmation.

    B __ Yes, that is the correct way.

5 Which documents need to be faxed?

    A __ The ones that are in this folder.

    B __ Please write this down.

Listening

5 🎧 Listen to a conversation between a new secretary and an office manager. Mark the following statements as true (T) or false (F).

1 __ The woman has tried sending the fax more than once.

2 __ The fax machine is broken.

3 __ The woman has seen this problem before.

6 🎧 Listen again and complete the conversation.

Secretary:	Oh, so you're sure you have the right 1 _____ _____?
Employee:	Yes, I've gotten a 2 _____ each time. But it's always blank pages that get sent.
Secretary:	I see. Well, I'm pretty sure I know what the problem is.
Employee:	Great! What's 3 _____ _____?
Secretary:	You have to insert the pages 4 _____ _____ _____ . I think you've been putting them in the 5 _____ _____ .
Employee:	That would explain the blank pages. What an embarrassing mistake!
Secretary:	Don't worry. It 6 _____ _____ _____ _____ .

Speaking

7 With a partner, act out the roles below, based on the dialogue from Task 6. Then switch roles.

USE LANGUAGE SUCH AS:

I think the fax machine is broken.

When I send the fax, my client gets blank pages.

I'm pretty sure I know what the problem is.

Student A: Help Student B find out why his or her fax is not going through correctly. Talk about:

- the problem
- fax number
- solution

Student B: You are having trouble sending a fax. Ask Student A for help.

Writing

8 You are a secretary. Use the conversation from Task 7 and the poster to write a sheet that helps people avoid mistakes with the fax machine. Talk about:

- Fax numbers
- Confirmation
- Inserting pages

_____

_____

_____

_____

_____

_____

board

chat

THURSDAY 18TH MAY

Morning:
- Departmental Meeting, 10 am, room 194
- **Update** staff on new company structure
- **Address** staff problems from changes to company structure.

Afternoon:
- ~~Lunch Meeting with Roy Johnstone to discuss health and safety. 12.30, Director's Restaurant.~~ **POSTPONED.** Now 22nd May, 1pm.
- **Chat** with Celine Stengle about information for new employees. Level 3 Meeting Room
- **Set up** an **induction** meeting for all new employees in mid June. Ask Celine for their contact details.
- Sales Team Meeting at 3:00
  Agenda: Discuss reasons for last year's poor sales
  Brainstorm new marketing ideas

Evening:
- Dinner with the **board** of directors to discuss financial issues relating to the new site. 7:30 pm, Legacy Restaurant

Notes:
- Remember to **cancel** the meeting with Tomako Yutsihiro, (May 31st) because it **clashes** with the company's **AGM**.
- **Arrange** a meeting with Clement Yee to discuss last year's sales.

Get ready!

❶ **Before you read the passage, talk about these questions.**

1 How has technology changed the way businesses have meetings?

2 What can make a meeting successful or unsuccessful?

Reading

❷ 🎧 **Listen and read the extract from the manager's planner. Then, choose the correct answer. What will the manager talk to the sales team about?**

1 Who will the manager NOT meet on Thursday?
   A Roy Johnstone
   B Celine Stengle
   C the sales team
   D the board of directors

2 What can be inferred about the company?
   A It had good sales the previous year.
   B It recently hired new workers.
   C It is closing its old site.
   D It makes safety equipment.

3 When will the manager discuss financial issues?
   A in the morning   C in the afternoon
   B at lunchtime   D in the evening

Vocabulary

❸ **Read the sentences and choose the correct meaning of the underlined words.**

1 The company is having its <u>AGM</u> on Thursday.
   A Associated Growers Meet
   B Annual General Meeting
   C Administration Governance Meeting

2 New staff members must attend an <u>induction meeting</u>.
   A a meeting to discuss employee problems
   B a meeting to introduce staff to the company
   C a meeting to brainstorm new ideas

3 An hour is long enough to have a <u>chat</u>.
   A brief talk   B formal meeting
   C argument

4 The problem was <u>addressed</u> by the manager.
   A discussed   B forgotten
   C written down

4 **Place a check (✓) next to the response that answers the question.**

1 Can you arrange a meeting with the team?

    A __ Yes, I'll set it up.

    B __ Yes, I'll cancel it.

2 The appointment clashes with her board meeting.

    A __ OK, well we can postpone it.

    B __ Great! See you at the meeting!

3 Will you tell the staff about the changes?

    A __ Yes, I'll brainstorm some ideas.

    B __ Yes, I'll update them.

Listening

5 🎧 **Listen to a phone call between two co-workers. Then mark the following statements as true (T) or false (F).**

1 __ The woman cannot attend the morning meeting.

2 __ The man will explain the new policies alone.

3 __ The woman will explain her summaries to the staff.

6 🎧 **Listen again and complete the conversation.**

Employee 2:	Hi Derek, it's Liz. Is there any way we can **1** _____ the meeting this morning?
Employee 1:	I don't think so. We need to **2** _____ the staff on the new company policies.
Employee 2:	I only want to postpone it until this afternoon. **3** _____ _____ three o'clock?
Employee 1:	No, I have another meeting then. Why do you want to change it anyway?
Employee 2:	It **4** _____ _____ my meeting with the board of directors. I'm sorry, I only just realized it.
Employee 1:	Well, I guess I can **5** _____ _____ _____ _____ .
Employee 2:	Is that okay? I can **6** _____ _____ all of my summaries.

Speaking

7 **With a partner, act out the roles below, based on the dialogue from Task 6. Then switch roles.**

Student A: You need to change the time of a meeting. Talk to Student B about:

● setting a new time

● reason for change

● meeting material

Make up some personal details and a time to postpone the meeting until.

Student B: Talk to Student A about changing the time of a meeting and who will run it.

Writing

8 **You are a manager. Use the conversation from Task 7 to write a memo to your team to postpone a meeting. Talk about:**

● When and where the meeting was originally

● When and where the new meeting will be

● What you want to discuss in the meeting

_____

_____

_____

_____

_____

_____

_____

_____

_____

objection

bicker

state your opinion

send your apologies

Get ready!

1 **Before you read the passage, talk about these questions.**

1 What are the challenges and responsibilities of running a meeting?

2 What are some behaviors that would be considered rude at a meeting?

Reading

2 **Read the blog from a business website. Then, read the summary of the dialogue. Fill in the blanks with the correct words from the word bank.**

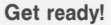 **BANK**

attend   common
unproductive   state

The writer believes that meetings are **1** _____ because people argue and don't listen. The writer recommends that people say sorry if they cannot **2** _____ a meeting. They should **3** _____ their opinions just once and use **4** _____ language.

APRIL 9th

Business blog

MEETING ETIQUETTE – BE POLITE, BE PRODUCTIVE!

Some meetings are really unproductive. People **bicker** – they **talk over** others and don't listen. Consequently, meetings drag on and on. This wouldn't happen if businesses had a set of meeting rules. Instead, meetings would be useful, productive and short! Here are my suggestions for meeting etiquette.

- **Send your apologies** if you cannot attend. Your colleagues may be waiting for you so they can start the meeting.

- **State your opinion** once only. If it's a good idea, people will **take note**. There's no need to **repeat yourself**.

- If you **disagree** with someone, don't **interrupt**. Wait until the other person finishes speaking, and then state your **objection**.

- Don't use **jargon**. Your colleagues may not be specialists in your field, so they will need to keep **asking for explanations**. This **wastes time**. Talk in everyday language so that everybody can understand.

Vocabulary

3 **Choose the word that is closest in meaning to the underlined part.**

1 Write a message saying sorry if you cannot attend.

  A State your opinion

  B Send your apologies

  C Ask for an explanation

2 It is unprofessional to argue in an immature way during meetings.

  A interrupt   **B** disagree   **C** bicker

3 It's rude to talk when other people are talking.

  A repeat yourself

  B talk over other people

  C take note of other people

4 During meetings Jane says the same thing again and again.

  A repeats herself   **B** disagrees   **C** interrupts

4 Read the sentence pairs. Choose where the words best fit in the blanks.

1 **objection / jargon**

Does anyone have a(n) _____ to this suggestion?

_____ should only be used if everyone understands it.

2 **waste time / take note**

_____ of any important changes.

Don't _____ arguing.

3 **ask for an explanation / state your opinion**

It is important to _____ if the material is confusing.

Please do not _____ until the chairman invites you to do so.

5 🎧 Listen and read the text again. What did you learn about meeting etiquette?

Listening

6 🎧 Listen to a conversation between an employee and a manager. Mark the following statements as true (T) or false (F).

1 ___ The woman feels the meetings are not productive.

2 ___ The man wants people to speak less in meetings.

3 ___ The man will write a set of rules for meetings.

7 🎧 Listen again and complete the conversation.

Employee:	It's these meetings. They're really getting 1 _____ _____ _____ .
Manager:	What do you mean?
Employee:	People always 2 _____ _____ _____ . It wastes so much time.
Manager:	I disagree. I want to 3 _____ people to speak if they have an objection.
Employee:	That's good. But they shouldn't 4 _____ _____ other people or repeat themselves over and over.
Manager:	Okay, I agree with that.
Employee:	Also, it might help if we asked the engineers to use less 5 _____ . We lose a lot of time just asking what certain words mean.
Manager:	Maybe we need to 6 _____ _____ some guidelines for meeting etiquette.

Speaking

8 With a partner, act out the roles below, based on the dialogue from Task 7. Then switch roles.

USE LANGUAGE SUCH AS:

It wastes so much time.

We lose a lot of time …

Maybe we need to …

Student A: You have ideas to improve meetings. Talk to Student B about:

● use of time

● problems and behaviors

● suggestions

Student B: You are a manager. Talk to Student A about improving meetings.

Writing

9 You are a manager. Use the conversation from Task 8 and the blog to write new meeting etiquette guidelines for your team (100-120 words). Talk about:

● What staff should do if they cannot attend a meeting

● What staff should do if they have an objection

● What language staff should use in meetings

_____

_____

_____

_____

audience

memo

Dear Team,

As you know, you are all making presentations for potential new investors next week. Please take the time to review the following guidelines – we need these presentations to be organized, accurate and professional.

- Start by **introducing** yourself and your subject. **Outline** the different sections of your presentation.

- When you finish a **section**, **summarize** it. Make it clear that you are **moving on to** a new section.

- Use **diagrams** where possible. You can show these on **handouts** or on **slides**. Refer to them in the presentation using phrases such as "As you can see in the diagram..."

- At the end, tell the **audience** you're finished and invite them to ask questions.

- Don't read your presentation from your **notes**. You need to maintain **eye contact** with the audience.

- **Prepare** and practice with your co-workers! Make helpful suggestions to each other before the big day!

Good luck!
Janice

Get ready!

1 **Before you read the passage, talk about these questions.**

1 What do you think is the most difficult part of giving a presentation?

2 What makes a presentation great? What makes a presentation bad?

Reading

2 🎧 **Listen and read the memo about an upcoming presentation. Then, mark the following statements as true (T) or false (F). How should someone make a presentation?**

1 __ The presentations will update current investors about profits.

2 __ The manager directs the team to provide several summaries.

3 __ Presenters should refer to notes often to guarantee accurate information.

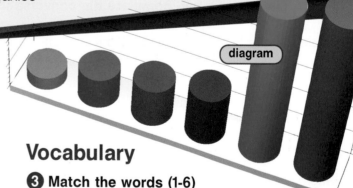

diagram

Vocabulary

3 **Match the words (1-6) with the definitions (A-F).**

1 __ introduce   4 __ summarize

2 __ outline   5 __ move on

3 __ eye contact   6 __ prepare

A to change to a different topic

B to repeat the most important points or facts

C to get ready

D to tell someone a person's name when they meet

E to give the main ideas without all the details

F the act of looking someone else in the eyes

4 Choose the correct word pairs to fill in the blanks.

1 Make your ____ more attractive by including ____ .
   A slides – notes   B handouts – diagrams
   C notes – sections

2 Presenters should look at their ____, not the ____ .
   A audience – notes   B slides – notes
   C handouts – diagrams

3 Each ____ needs to be presented on a different ____ .
   A diagram – audience   B handout – section
   C section – slide

Listening

5 🎧 Listen to a conversation between two co-workers. Check (✓) the parts of the man's presentation that need improvement.

1 ☐ the introduction   4 ☐ the diagrams
2 ☐ eye contact   5 ☐ the outline
3 ☐ moving between sections

6 🎧 Listen again and complete the conversation.

Employee 2: It was good. I liked how you **1** _____ _____ . And you **2** _____ the different sections of the presentation well.

Employee 1: Thanks. Any other strengths?

Employee 2: You maintained **3** _____ _____ . That's very important. But it was difficult to know when you **4** _____ _____ .

Employee 1: What do you mean?

Employee 2: Well, you never stopped and summarized. For instance, one minute you were talking about first quarter profits, and the next you were onto reducing costs.

Employee 1: I see. So just stop and go over things once in a while?

Employee 2: Exactly. Also, the **5** _____ are a little confusing.

Employee 1: Really? How so?

Employee 2: There's just so much information. Maybe you could **6** _____ them.

Speaking

7 With a partner, act out the roles below, based on the dialogue from Task 6. Then switch roles.

USE LANGUAGE SUCH AS:

What did you think of my presentation?
I liked how you …
Maybe you could …

Student A: You are helping a co-worker prepare for a presentation. Talk to Student B about his or her:
● strengths
● parts to improve
Make up something the presenter didn't summarise.

Student B: You are preparing for a presentation. Talk to Student A about it.

Writing

8 You are a preparing for a presentation. Use the conversation from Task 7 to write notes on your presentation (100-120 words). Make sure to answer the following questions:

● What you do well
● What you need to improve

_____
_____
_____
_____

Get ready!

1 Before you read the passage, talk about these questions.

1   What tools do people use to help them manage their time?

2   Do you think employees waste too much time on the Internet? How can this be prevented?

Business TIMEKEEPING
Seminar with Keith Tyler
Wednesday 3:00 pm, Conference Room C

Are you always trying to **make up for lost time**? Do you sometimes feel there are not enough hours in the day?

If you said "yes", your business might be suffering. You can't run a business **behind schedule**, or you'll **delay** sales and lose profits. You can't be late when making payments or you'll lose your best suppliers. And you can't set new **deadlines** for the **completion** of your projects or you'll discourage investors.

Come to Keith Tyler's seminar on Business Timekeeping and learn the secrets of how to **keep track** of your workload. Learn how to **prioritize** and set realistic deadlines. Find out the best ways to **delegate** work to other people or other businesses. Learn how you can minimize **distractions** and **interruptions** and maximize your concentration levels. With these handy tips, your business will soon run efficiently and **ahead of schedule**.

Reading

2 🎧 Listen and read the brochure advertising a seminar. Then, complete the table using information from the passage. Use the completed table to say why someone should attend the meeting.

Disadvantages of bad time-keeping	A	It can delay sales
	B	You will 1 _____
	C	You will 2 _____
What you will learn	A	How to keep track of your workload
	B	How to 3 _____
	C	How to delegate
	D	How to 4 _____

Vocabulary

3 Match the words (1-6) with the definitions (A-F).

1 __ distraction   4 __ delegate
2 __ interruption   5 __ delay
3 __ completion   6 __ prioritize

A   to give some of your work to someone else

B   the act of finishing a job or activity

C   to order things based on importance

D   something that prevents concentration

E   something that stops a person who was talking or working

F   to make something happen later than planned

4 Check (✓) the sentence that uses the underlined part correctly.

1 __ **A** A calendar <u>keeps track</u> of appointments.
  __ **B** A good business is always <u>behind schedule</u>.

2 __ **A** Late workers rarely have to <u>make up for lost time</u>.
  __ **B** Companies <u>set a deadline</u> when they start a project.

3 __ **A** Distractions help people stay <u>ahead of schedule</u>.
  __ **B** Delegating work helps managers with <u>timekeeping</u>.

Listening

5 🎧 Listen to a conversation between the seminar speaker and an audience member. Mark the following statements as true (T) or false (F).

1 __ The woman is a small business owner.
2 __ The man recommends setting deadlines close to one another.
3 __ The man suggests the woman complete the smallest jobs first.

6 🎧 Listen again and complete the conversation.

Speaker: I'm glad to hear it. Are you a **1** _____ _____ _____?
Woman: I am, and I have a lot of the problems you talked about: late deadlines, losing sales.
Speaker: Hopefully this will help you **2** _____ _____ _____ things.
Woman: I hope so. But I do have a question about setting priorities.
Speaker: Let's hear it. Maybe it will improve my presentation.
Woman: Well, let's say I have multiple deadlines set for the same time period. How do I **3** _____ them?
Speaker: That's difficult. First, I'd say spread the **4** _____ out.
Woman: Oh, I definitely will from now on.
Speaker: Good, good. But as for the deadlines you already have, I'd prioritize them by their **5** _____ _____ .

Speaking

7 With a partner, act out the roles below, based on the dialogue from Task 6. Then switch roles.

USE LANGUAGE SUCH AS:

I thought that was a wonderful seminar.

I do have a question about setting priorities.

Just complete the jobs that ... first.

Student A: You have attended a seminar on time management. Ask the speaker for advice. Talk to Student B about:
● the seminar
● setting priorities
● multiple deadlines

Student B: You are a speaker at a seminar on time management. Answer Student A's questions and give advice.

Writing

8 You are a seminar speaker. Use the conversation from Task 7 to write notes about improving your seminar. Talk about:

● How to schedule deadlines
● How to prioritize multiple deadlines

_____
_____
_____
_____

negotiate

parties

back down

close a deal

Business World | Issue 65

TIPS for Better Negotiations

BY HELEN ROBERTS

Your working life is full of negotiations. You don't just **negotiate** with other companies. You negotiate whenever there are two **parties** with different needs. And even though everyone involved wants to find a **compromise** that is **mutually acceptable**, many people dislike negotiating because of the **conflicting interests**.

But negotiations need not be **confrontational**. Don't try to win a negotiation. If you treat it as a contest, you will create a **hostile** atmosphere. Respect the other person and try to understand his or her needs. This way, you can create a spirit of cooperation.

Sometimes, the other party may reject your suggestions, and you need to **anticipate** this. A negotiation is a **trade-off**, and sometimes you will need to **back down**. So prepare alternative options in case your preferred solution is unacceptable. Finally, don't negotiate if you are tired or stressed. You will never **close the deal** when negotiations are too **intense**. Reschedule to another time.

Get ready!

❶ **Before you read the passage, talk about these questions.**

1 How can negotiations help or harm a business?

2 What are some qualities of a good negotiator?

Reading

❷ 🎧 **Listen and read the article in the business magazine. Then, mark the following statements as true (T) or false (F). When should you not negotiate?**

1 __ A good negotiator wins each part of a negotiation.

2 __ Successful negotiations do not always end with ideal outcomes.

3 __ Changing negotiation times can help people compromise.

Vocabulary

❸ **Choose the word that is closest in meaning to the underlined part.**

1 Just <u>stop demanding</u> what you want.

   A anticipate   B back down   C close the deal

2 The parties are very <u>eager to argue with each other</u>.

   A intense   B mutually acceptable

   C confrontational

3 Mr. Brown will offer a deal, so try to <u>think about it beforehand</u>.

   A anticipate it   B close the deal   C negotiate

4 Try to <u>discuss and change</u> the contract terms.

   A close the deal   B anticipate   C negotiate

5 <u>Give up something in order to get something more important</u> if you have to.

   A trade-off   B party   C interest

4 Match the words (1-7) with the definitions (A-G).

1 __ hostile
2 __ intense
3 __ conflicting interest
4 __ mutually acceptable
5 __ deal
6 __ compromise
7 __ party

A an agreement
B being competitive and eager to argue
C a person or group in a negotiation
D being satisfactory to both sides of a negotiation
E a solution in which both sides of a negotiation give up something
F a point of a negotiation which both sides consider very important
G being extremely stressful

Listening

5 🎧 **Listen to a conversation between two employees. Then answer the questions.**

1 What can you infer about the woman?
  A She has not negotiated before.
  B She will not accept the current prices.
  C She has offered several trade-offs.
  D She did not anticipate higher prices.

2 What compromise does the man suggest?
  A purchasing the paper at full price
  B allowing the suppliers to delay delivery
  C buying a large amount of paper at once
  D paying a portion of the transportation costs

6 🎧 **Listen again and complete the conversation.**

M: How is the negotiation with the paper suppliers going?
W: It's intense. They won't drop their prices.
M: Well, we **1** _____ that. Their transportation costs are much higher these days.
W: But if they don't **2** _____ _____, we'll never close the deal.
M: Have you offered a **3** _____?
W: Not yet. I can't think of anything that we can give up.
M: Think of it from their point of view. They can't lower their prices because of transportation costs.
W: Exactly.
M: So what if we offer to **4** _____ _____ _____ _____ of paper at once?
W: How would that help us?
M: They'll only have to deliver it once, which will **5** _____ _____ on their transportation costs.

Speaking

7 With a partner, act out the roles below, based on the dialogue from Task 6. Then switch roles.

USE LANGUAGE SUCH AS:

How is the negotiation with ... going?

Think of it from their point of view.

How would that help us?

Student A: Student B is having problems with a negotiation. Give advice about:
● anticipating problems
● offering compromise
● how to lower prices
Make up a type of supplier.

Student B: You are having trouble negotiating with suppliers. Ask Student A for advice.

Writing

8 You are a manager. Use the conversation from Task 7 and the article to write advice for a co-worker who is leading a negotiation for the first time. Talk about:

● How to treat the people in the other party
● What to do before the negotiation
● What to do in order to close the deal

_____
_____
_____
_____
_____

13 Customer service

ADventure TRAVEL LTD

repeat business

Get ready!

1 Before you read the passage, talk about these questions.

1 Why can working in customer service be challenging or frustrating?

2 Have you had a bad experience with customer service? What happened, and how could it have been better?

Reading

2 🎧 Listen and read the extract from an employee manual. Then, read the summary of the passage. Fill in the blanks with the correct words from the word bank. What kind of staff do customers appreciate?

BANK

feedback	reliable
recommend	**satisfaction**

The employee manual states that customer 1 _____ is very important. This is because it gets a lot of business from customers who 2 _____ the company to their friends. In order to keep customers happy, the company pays attention to their 3 _____ . It also encourages workers to be helpful and 4 _____ .

ADventure TRAVEL LTD

Employee Manual
5.4 Customer Service

Customer **satisfaction** is the most important feature of our business. Our success depends on customer **loyalty**. We rely on repeat business, and many of our new customers come to us through **word of mouth recommendations**. We can only maintain this **customer base** if we continually meet, or preferably **exceed,** customer **expectations**. To accomplish this, our company has two policies:

5.4.1 We value feedback

When a customer complains, do not be offended. They are pointing out something that we can improve. Thank them for **bringing this problem to our attention**. Assure them that you will **rectify** it as soon as possible.

5.4.2 We go the extra mile

All staff should be prepared to **go beyond the call of duty**. Customers appreciate helpful, reliable staff, and they appreciate it when they receive something extra. So always **go out of your way** to fulfill customers' needs.

satisfaction

go out of your way

Vocabulary

3 Check (✓) the sentence that uses the underlined part correctly.

1 __ **A** Employees should ask customers to <u>rectify</u> problems.

__ **B** A company with a large <u>customer base</u> has high customer satisfaction.

2 __ **A** Employees who <u>go beyond the call of duty</u> are appreciated.

__ **B** <u>Word-of-mouth recommendations</u> are bad for a business.

3 __ **A** Bosses don't like employees who <u>go the extra mile</u>.

__ **B** If you see a problem, <u>bring it to the boss's attention</u>.

4 Write a word that is similar in meaning to the underlined part.

1 I <u>promise</u> you that I will solve this problem. a _ _ u _ _

2 Your reports <u>are better than I thought they would be</u>.
_ x _ e _ _   e _ _ e _ t _ t _ _ _ s

3 The client's <u>happiness with our service</u> is key.
s _ t _ s _ _ _ _ i _ _

4 <u>Use extra effort</u> to make the customer happy.
g _   o _ _   _ f   y _ _ _   _ a _

5 A customer's <u>choice to remain with one company</u> is hard to earn.
l _ y _ _ _ _

6 The company asks for <u>opinions about its service</u>.
_ e _ _ b _ _ k

Listening

5 🎧 **Listen to a conversation between a hotel manager and an employee. Then answer the questions.**

1 What is the main idea of the conversation?
A the man's performance at work
B negative feedback about the hotel
C steps to increase customer loyalty
D additions to the man's responsibilities

2 What can you infer about the man?
A He has asked for raises in the past.
B He is remembered by hotel guests.
C He accidentally offended a customer.
D He will be promoted to manager.

6 🎧 **Listen again and complete the conversation.**

Manager: Well, you understand how important **1** _____ _____ is here at the Regal Inn.

Employee: Of course. Did I offend a customer?

Manager: No, no, just the opposite. It's been **2** _____ _____ _____ _____ that your name comes up frequently in positive customer feedback.

Employee: Oh, good. But I'm just doing my job, really.

Manager: That's not what I hear. Making calls for guests and helping them get tickets to shows – you're going **3** _____ _____ _____ _____ to make sure customers are satisfied.

Employee: It's not that much, really.

Manager: Still, the business from **4** _____ _____ _____ _____ you're bringing in means a lot to us. So we're giving you a **5** _____ .

Speaking

7 **With a partner, act out the roles below, based on the dialogue from Task 6. Then switch roles.**

USE LANGUAGE SUCH AS:

You wanted to see me?

Did I offend a customer?

That's not what I hear.

Student A: You are a hotel manager. An employee has been mentioned in customer feedback. Talk to Student B about:
● customer satisfaction
● feedback
● result of employee's actions
Make up a name for a hotel.

Student B: You are an employee at a hotel. Answer Student A's questions.

Writing

8 **You are a manager. Use the conversation from Task 7 and the employee manual to write an employee profile for the company newsletter (100-120 words). Make up a name for the employee. Include:**

● The importance of customer loyalty
● What the employee does well
● How the employee was rewarded

_____
_____
_____
_____
_____
_____

Dear Mr. Tyler,

I am pleased to **confirm** your **itinerary** for your trip from Sydney to London.

I have booked you on a **business class** flight SQ174 from Sydney Airport to London Heathrow. Departure is at 8:05 am on August 19th. This includes a 19-hour **layover** in Singapore.

I arranged **accommodations** at the Singapore Orchid Hotel, which has a wide range of luxury **amenities**. You will arrive at London Heathrow at 3:55 pm on August 20th. Your **e-ticket** is attached to this mail.

On arrival at Heathrow you can reach the center of London either by train or **coach**. **First class** train **fares** start at £26. Alternatively you can **rent** a car at the airport. Please let me know your preference so I can make the necessary **reservations**.

Thank you once again for choosing Merit Travel. If you have any other queries, please do not hesitate to get in touch.

Jana Lemon
Merit Travel

Get ready!

❶ Before you read the passage, talk about these questions.

1 Do you think the Internet will make business travel unnecessary? Why or why not?

2 What are the benefits and challenges of business travel?

Reading

❷ 🎧 Listen and read the email message from a travel agency. Then, choose the correct answers. What should Mr. Tyler do if he has any queries?

1 Which of the following is NOT on Mr. Tyler's itinerary?

   A a layover in Singapore

   B a flight from Sydney to London

   C accommodations in a luxury hotel

   D a coach ticket to central London

2 What is the main idea of the passage?

   A the details of an upcoming trip

   B a description of destination options

   C the estimated cost of a vacation

   D services provided by a travel agency

3 What is included with the email?

   A a flight ticket

   B a hotel booking form

   C a train schedule

   D a list of car rental agencies

Vocabulary

❸ Match the words (1-7) with the definitions (A-G).

1 __ itinerary   5 __ reservation

2 __ layover   6 __ coach

3 __ e-ticket   7 __ business class

4 __ accommodations

A a comfortable bus for longer journeys

B a place where travelers can stay

C an electronic pass to board a plane

D an agreement that something will be held

E a stop mid-way through a journey

F a detailed plan of a journey

G a large, expensive seating area

4 Fill in the blanks with the correct words and phrases from the word bank.

word BANK

rent   first class   fare   arrival   amenities

1 Businesspeople fly _____ because it is more comfortable.
2 The train _____ from this city to the capital is very expensive.
3 The hotel has several _____, such as a swimming pool.
4 Upon _____, passengers should go to baggage claim.
5 Carol will _____ a car while she is on business in New York.

Listening

5 🎧 Listen to a conversation between a travel agent and a businessman. Check (✓) the costs that the travel agent must investigate.

1 ❏ business class flights to London
2 ❏ accommodations in Singapore
3 ❏ coach fares from Heathrow to London
4 ❏ renting a car in London
5 ❏ accommodations in London

6 🎧 Listen again and complete the conversation.

Agent:	Oh hello Mr. Tyler. Did you receive the **1** _____?
Businessman:	Yes I did, thank you. But I had one or two questions.
Agent:	Sure, fire away.
Businessman:	Firstly, about the **2** _____ in Singapore. Are the **3** _____ included in the price of the airline ticket?
Agent:	Yes it is. It's part of the **4** _____ _____ package.
Businessman:	That's great. Secondly, how much are **5** _____ _____ from Heathrow to the center of London?
Agent:	I can find that out for you.
Businessman:	That'd be great. Can you also find out the cost of **6** _____ a car for five days too, please?

Speaking

7 With a partner, act out the roles below, based on the dialogue from Task 6. Then switch roles.

USE LANGUAGE SUCH AS:

Did you receive the itinerary?
I had one or two questions.
Can you also find out …

Student A: You received your itinerary for a business trip. Ask Student B about:

● cost of accommodations
● transportation options and costs

Make up a destination.

Student B: You are a travel agent. Answer Student A's questions.

Writing

8 You are a travel agent. Use the conversation from Task 7 and the email to write an email to a client explaining the reservations you have made. Talk about:

● Where the client is traveling to
● How the client will get there
● What accommodations and transportation options you have arranged

_____
_____
_____
_____
_____

Information ?i

Currency Exchange

Get ready!

1 Before you read the passage, talk about these questions.

1 What can a traveler do if he or she loses a passport?
2 What other things do you need to take with you on a business trip?

passport

map

TRAVEL ESSENTIALS

You're going on a business trip abroad. You're about to leave your house when you think 'Did I forget anything?' Does this sound familiar? Use this checklist to ensure you don't forget anything important!

- Don't forget your **passport**! Keep it with you at all times, but be careful that it doesn't fall out of your bag or pocket or get stolen.
- Do you have the **paperwork** relating to your **journey**? You'll need your flight number when you **check in**.
- Have you got any **foreign currency**? You don't want to be stuck abroad with no money!
- Do you take **medication** regularly? If so, don't forget it! Also remember that in some countries, you will need **inoculations** before you travel.

Where will you go when you arrive? Take a **travel guide** or a **map** of your **destination**. It's also a good idea to have your hotel's **contact information** handy. You may need it when filling out forms.

currency

medication

Vocabulary

3 Write a word that is similar in meaning to the underlined part.

1 You need several <u>injections that prevent the spread of disease</u>.
_ n _ _ _ l _ _ _ o _ _

2 Be sure that you bring any <u>drugs prescribed by a doctor</u>.
_ _ d _ _ _ _ i _ _

3 The airline recommends that passengers arrive early to <u>register for their flight</u>. _ _ e _ _ - _ n

4 Visitors may not enter without a <u>document that provides identification</u>. _ _ s _ _ o _ _

5 Keep the hotel's <u>phone number and address</u> with you.
c _ _ t _ _ _ i _ _ _ _ m _ _ _ o _

6 Do you have a <u>paper displaying streets and major attractions</u> of the city? _ a _

7 The <u>trip</u> across the ocean is much faster than it used to be.
j _ _ r _ _ y

8 Read a <u>book with information about an area</u> before leaving.
_ r _ _ e _ _ _ i _ _

Reading

2 🎧 Listen and read the extract from a travel guide. Then, mark the following statements as true (T) or false (F). What should you have with you while on a business trip?

1 _ Important documents should be stored in baggage.

2 _ Travelers should change money before leaving.

3 _ Some countries require visitors to get shots when they arrive.

④ Read the sentence and choose the correct meaning of the underlined words.

1 Traveling to another country involves a lot of <u>paperwork</u>.

   A problems **B** documents **C** identification

2 John finally reached his <u>destination</u>.

   A the place where someone lives

   B the place someone is traveling to

   C a town which has an airport

3 Tina needs some <u>foreign currency</u>.

   A money from another country

   B information about the area

   C help from the airport staff

Listening

⑤ 🎧 **Listen to a conversation between a businessman and his personal assistant. Choose the correct answers.**

1 Where is the man's map?

   A in his bag **C** in his travel guide

   B in his jacket **D** in his pocket

2 What is the man likely to do next?

   A take a taxi to the airport **C** purchase a travel guide

   B get foreign currency **D** check in for his flight

⑥ 🎧 **Listen again and complete the conversation.**

Businessman:	Yes, they're **1** _____ _____ _____ somewhere.
Assistant:	You should take them out. It will make your **2** _____-_____ a lot faster.
Businessman:	Good thinking. I'll keep them **3** _____ _____ _____ .
Assistant:	Also, I put the **4** _____ _____ _____ _____ _____ in your travel guide.
Businessman:	Great, thanks.
Assistant:	And did you ever grab any **5** _____?
Businessman:	I don't need any. I have my credit card. I'll **6** _____ _____ _____ _____ when I arrive.
Assistant:	Are you sure about that? Don't you need to take a taxi from the airport?
Businessman:	I was planning on it. Why do you ask?
Assistant:	Well they only accept cash.

Speaking

⑦ **With a partner, act out the roles below, based on the dialogue from Task 6. Then switch roles.**

USE LANGUAGE SUCH AS:

Do you have everything you need?

You should take them out.

Don't you need to …?

Student A: Your boss is taking an international trip. Make sure Student B has:

● necessary paperwork

● information about destination

● currency

Student B: Talk to Student A about what items you have or need for the trip.

Writing

⑧ **You are a personal assistant. Use the conversation from Task 7 and the travel guide to write a list of items your boss needs for a trip. Include:**

● paperwork

● information about the destination

● money

● medicine

_____

_____

_____

_____

_____

_____

Glossary

@ symbol [N-COUNT-U5] The @ **symbol** separates the name from the location in the email address.

accommodation [N UNCOUNT-U14] **Accommodation** is a place where travelers can live or stay.

account [N-COUNT-U5] An **account** is the subscription to the company that provides an email address.

address [V-T-U8] To **address** a problem means to deal with it.

AGM [N-COUNT-U8] An **AGM** is an annual general meeting.

ahead of schedule [ADJ PHRASE-U11] If you are **ahead of schedule**, you have finished your work earlier than expected.

amenity [N COUNT-U14] An **amenity** is something that will make guests' lives more comfortable or pleasant, such as a shop, restaurant or swimming pool.

anticipate [V-T-U12] To **anticipate** something is to realize that it may happen and prepare for it.

arrange [V-T-U8] To **arrange** something means to organize it.

assembled [V-I -U1] When pieces of something are put together they are **assembled**.

assure [V-T-U13] To **assure** someone means to promise action.

attachment [N-COUNT-U5] An **attachment** is a file that is sent along with an email.

audience [N COUNT-U10] An **audience** is a group of people who watch something.

back down [PHRASAL V-U12] To **back down** means to stop arguing for something you want.

beginning [N-COUNT-U6] The **beginning** of a letter is the start that addresses the recipient.

behind schedule [ADJ PHRASE-U11] If you are **behind schedule**, you are late in completing your plans.

benefits [N-COUNT-U1] The good or helpful qualities of something are its **benefits**.

bicker [V-I-U9] To **bicker** means to argue in an immature way.

board [N-COUNT-U8] A **board** is a committee who decides major issues.

brainstorm [V-I-U8] To **brainstorm** means to come up with lots of ideas.

bring something to someone's attention [V PHRASE-U13] If you **bring something to someone's attention**, you inform someone about something.

business class [ADJ-U14] **Business class** is an expensive seating area on some flights that has more room than average seats but less room than first class.

can you connect me to extension … [PHRASE-U4] Ask for a telephone extension number by saying. "**can you connect me to extension …**"

cancel [V-T-U8] To **cancel** something means to stop a plan for an appointment or meeting.

catalogue [N-COUNT-U2] A **catalogue** is a magazine with photos and descriptions of products for sale.

chat [N-COUNT-U8] A **chat** is an informal talk.

check in [PHRASAL V-U15] To **check in** means to register for your flight. You check in when you arrive at an airport.

clash [V-I-U8] When two appointments **clash**, they both happen at the same time.

close a deal [V PHRASE-U12] To **close a deal** means to come to an agreement.

closing remarks [N-COUNT-U6] The **closing remarks** are the part of a letter that comes just before the ending.

coach [N COUNT-U14] A **coach** is similar to a bus, but it is more comfortable and driven longer distances.

come out [V-I-U1] When a company **comes out** with a new item, it has just become available for sale.

completion [N UNCOUNT-U11] **Completion** is the act of finishing something.

compromise [N COUNT-U12] A **compromise** is an agreement in which people adapt their own desires to suit other people.

confirm [V-T-U14] To **confirm** something means to assure someone that something will happen.

confirmation [N-COUNT-U7] A sound or printout that indicates that a document has gone through correctly is a **confirmation**.

conflicting [ADJ-U12] If two things are **conflicting**, they disagree with each other.

confrontational [ADJ-U12] If someone is **confrontational**, he or she is aggressive towards another person.

contact information [N-UNCOUNT-U15] **Contact information** is the details that someone needs in order to phone or write to you.

could I speak to… [PHRASE-U4] To ask for the person you wish to speak with, say something like, "**could I speak to…**"

courtesy [N-COUNT-U4] **Courtesy** is the act of showing kindness and consideration.

cover sheet [N-COUNT-U7] The first page of a fax, containing all of the practical information is called the **cover sheet**.

currency [N-UNCOUNT-U15] **Currency** is the type of money used in a particular country.

customer base [N PHRASE-U13] A company's **customer base** are the customers who use the company's services.

customer service [N-UNCOUNT-U3] **Customer service** is the act of providing customers of a store with assistance.

customer service department [N-COUNT-U3] The **customer service department** is the place in a company where customers can get information and help with any problems or complaints.

delay [V-T-U11] To **delay** something means to make it late.

delegate [V-I-U11] To **delegate** means to give work to other people.

delete [V-I or T-U5] To **delete** a message is to remove it from an inbox.

destination [N-COUNT-U15] A **destination** is the place which you are traveling to.

developed [V-I-U1] A company has **developed** something when it has designed and built a new product.

diagram [N COUNT-U10] A **diagram** is a simple picture that helps you understand a process or change.

direct sales [N-UNCOUNT-U2] **Direct sales** is a system of marketing through independent salespeople instead of retailers.

disagree [V-I-U9] To **disagree** means to have a different opinion than someone else.

distraction [N COUNT-U11] A **distraction** is something which stops a person from concentrating on work.

distributed by [V-T-U1] An item is **distributed by** the company that gives or sells it.

documents [N-COUNT-U7] The pages used for official or professional purposes are often called **documents**.

e-commerce [N-UNCOUNT-U2] An online business sells products through the system of **e-commerce**.

email addresses [N-COUNT-U5] An **email address** is the unique place online where a person receives electronic mail.

enclosures [N-COUNT-U6] Items or documents that are included with a letter are listed as **enclosures**.

ending [N-COUNT-U6] The **ending** of the letter is a phrase before the signature that ends the letter.

e-ticket [N COUNT-U14] An **e-ticket** is a record of a ticket which has been booked electronically and can be printed.

exceed expectations [V PHRASE-U13] To **exceed expectations** means to do better than people thought you would do.

explanation [N-COUNT-U9] An **explanation** is a statement that helps people to understand something.

fare [N COUNT-U14] A **fare** is the cost of a trip on a specific type of transport.

fax number [N-COUNT-U7] The telephone number or code that is connected to the fax machine is the **fax number**.

fax something over [V-T-U7] When you send a fax, you can say that you will **fax something over**.

features [N-COUNT-U1] The special things that an item has or can do are its **features**.

feedback [N COUNT-U13] **Feedback** is a comment from a customer to a company about its service.

first class [ADJ-U14] **First class** is the most expensive and spacious seating area on flights and trains.

foreign [ADJ –U15] **Foreign** means from another country.

formal [ADJ-U5] If something is **formal**, it is impersonal, serious and follows established rules.

forward [V-I-U5] To **forward** a message is to send it on to another person.

go beyond the call of duty [V PHRASE-U13] To **go beyond the call of duty** means to do more work than your job states you must do.

go out of your way [V PHRASE-U13] To **go out of your way** to do something means to help someone by causing yourself some inconvenience.

go the extra mile [V PHRASE-U13] To **go the extra mile** means to do more work than expected in order to show your dedication.

go through [V-I-U7] When a fax is sent it is said to **go through** to the recipient's machine.

greeting [N-COUNT-U6] A **greeting** in a letter is a phrase that addresses the recipient.

guarantee [N-COUNT-U3] A **guarantee** is a promise that if something purchased does not work, it will be replaced, repaired or money refunded.

handout [N COUNT-U10] A **handout** is an informative piece of paper given out to the audience in presentations or classes.

hello, this is … [PHRASE-U4] A polite way to identify yourself on the telephone is to say, "**Hello, this is …**"

hostile [ADJ-U12] If someone is **hostile**, he or she is unfriendly and does not accept other people's opinions or ideas.

I will call you back on … [PHRASE-U4] Let a person know when you will call again by saying, "**I will call you back on …**"

I'm calling from… [PHRASE-U4] To identify a company, you can say, "**I'm calling from …**"

induction meeting [N-COUNT-U8] An **induction meeting** is a meeting to introduce people to a new job or project.

informal [ADJ-U5] If something is **informal**, it is personal, not serious and follows no set format or rules.

inoculation [N-COUNT-U15] An **inoculation** is a vaccination. It is an injection that prevents you from becoming ill.

insert [V-Tor I-U7] You **insert** the pages when you place them into the tray of the fax machine to be sent.

intense [ADJ-U9] If something is **intense**, it causes people to feel stressed.

interrupt [V-I-U9] To **interrupt** means to start talking when somebody is already talking.

interruption [N-COUNT-U11] An **interruption** is something that stops a person from working or speaking.

introduce yourself [V PHRASE-U10] To **introduce yourself** means to tell someone your name.

is…available? [PHRASE-U4] A way to ask for someone on the telephone is to ask, "**is … available?**"

item number [N-COUNT-U2] An **item number** is the special code that identifies a product.

itinerary [N COUNT-U14] An **itinerary** is a detailed list of your travel arrangements.

jargon [N-COUNT-U9] **Jargon** is language which is specific to a profession or an area of expertise.

journey [N-COUNT-U15] A **journey** is a long trip by car, bus, train or plane.

keep track [V PHRASE-U11] To **keep track** of something means to monitor or follow it.

keypad [N-COUNT-U7] The number pad that you use to dial a fax or phone number is called the **keypad**.

launched [V-I-U1] An item has been **launched** when a company begins to sell it.

layover [N-COUNT-U14] A **layover** is a stop on the way to a final destination.

loyalty [N UNCOUNT-U13] **Loyalty** is the act of staying with one service provider, not seeking a different one.

mail order [ADJ-U2] If a product is **mail order**, it is selected from catalogues, ordered by mail and shipped to the buyer.

maintain eye contact [V PHRASE-U10] To **maintain eye contact** means to look at people directly.

make [N-COUNT-U3] A **make** is the name of a company that produces a product.

make up for lost time [V PHRASE-U11] To **make up for lost time** means to do something quickly which was meant to be finished sooner.

manufactured [V-I-U1] When items are made or put together for sale they are **manufactured**.

map [N-COUNT-U15] A **map** is a plan of a town, area or country.

match [V-T-U2] To **match** a price means to sell it for the same amount as another store.

may I speak to … [PHRASE-U4] A way to ask for someone on the telephone is to ask "**May I speak to…**"

medication [N-UNCOUNT-U15] **Medication** is medicine you take regularly.

message [N-COUNT-U5] A **message** is the written information that is sent from one computer to another.

model number [N-COUNT-U3] A **model number** is a set of numbers on a product that identifies its features.

move on [PHRASAL V-U10] To **move on** means to change subject.

mutually acceptable [ADJ PHRASE-U12] If something is **mutually acceptable**, two or more parties are satisfied with it.

negotiate [V-I-U12] To **negotiate** means to discuss something to find a solution to a problem.

nice speaking to you [PHRASE- U4] At the end of a conversation, tell the person you enjoyed the talk, saying, "**nice speaking to you.**"

notes [PLURAL N-U10] **Notes** are papers that give information in brief.

objection [N-COUNT-U9] An **objection** is a comment which disagrees with another person's opinion.

Glossary

option [N-COUNT-U5] An **option** is a choice that can be taken or not.

outline [V-T-U10] To **outline** something means to briefly state the main features.

paperwork [N-UNCOUNT-U15] **Paperwork** is important information printed on paper.

party [N COUNT-U12] A **party** is a group of people who have the same interests.

passport [N-COUNT-U15] A **passport** is an important document which states your name and nationality. You need it when you travel to another country.

phone order [N-COUNT-U2] A **phone order** is an order for a product placed over the phone.

postpone [V-T-U8] To **postpone** something means to cancel an appointment and rearrange it for a later time.

prepare [V-I or T-U10] To **prepare** means to get ready for something.

prioritize [V-I-U11] To **prioritize** is to organize items in order of most important to least important.

promise [V-T-U2] To **promise** something is to tell someone that something is true or will happen.

quality [N-UNCOUNT-U1] The **quality** of something indicates how good or bad it is.

receipt [N-COUNT-U3] A **receipt** is a document that shows money was exchanged for a product.

recipient [N-COUNT-U6] The person who receives a letter is the **recipient**.

rectify [V-T-U13] To **rectify** a problem means to solve it.

refund [N-COUNT-U3] A **refund** is money that is returned to a buyer because he or she no longer wants the product.

rent [V-T or I-U14] To **rent** something means to pay to borrow something for a relatively short period of time.

repeat yourself [V PHRASE-U9] To **repeat yourself** means to say something several times.

replacement [N-COUNT-U3] A **replacement** is someone or something that takes the place of another.

reply to all [V-I-U5] To **reply to all** is to send a response to all of the addresses listed in an email.

resend [V-T or I-U7] If a fax does not go through the first time, you can **resend** it, by trying to send it to the same recipient a second time.

reservation [N COUNT-U14] A **reservation** is a booking.

retailer [N-COUNT-U2] A **retailer** sells products to consumers, usually through a store or web site.

return address [N-COUNT-U6] A **return address** is the address of a person who sends a letter.

salutation [N-COUNT-U6] A **salutation** is a phrase used to begin a letter.

satisfaction [N UNCOUNT-U13] **Satisfaction** is happiness with a company's service.

satisfied [ADJ-U3] If someone is **satisfied**, that person is pleased with someone or something.

section [N COUNT-U10] A **section** is one part of something.

send a fax [V PHRASE-T-U7] To **send a fax** is to send a copy of a document from one fax machine to another.

send your apologies [V PHRASE-U9] To **send your apologies** means to write a message saying sorry for not attending a meeting.

sender [N-COUNT-U6] The person who writes and mails the letter is the **sender**.

set a deadline [V PHRASE-U11] To **set a deadline** is to set a time when something will be finished.

set up [V-T-U8] To **set up** something means to arrange or organize.

shipped from [V-T-U1] When an item is **shipped from** a place it is mailed or sent from that location.

shipping [N-UNCOUNT-U2] The added cost to send an item that has been purchased is the **shipping** cost.

signature [N-COUNT-U6] A **signature** is the handwritten name of the sender of a letter, included at the bottom of the letter.

slide [N COUNT-U10] A **slide** is an image that is projected onto a screen.

state your opinion [V PHRASE-U9] To **state your opinion** means to say what you think.

subject [N-COUNT-U5] The **subject** is the title that gives information about the contents of a message.

summarize [V-I or T-U10] To **summarize** something means to repeat the main points that you mentioned earlier.

take note [V PHRASE-U9] To **take note** means to pay attention to something.

talk over someone [V PHRASE-U9] To **talk over someone** is to talk when he or she is speaking.

thank you for your time [PHRASE-U4] It is polite to thank a person for speaking with you by saying, "**Thank you for your time.**"

timekeeping [N UNCOUNT-U11] **Timekeeping** is the act of managing time.

trade-off [N COUNT-U12] A **trade-off** is a situation in which you lose something you want in order to gain something you want.

travel guide [N-COUNT-U15] A **travel guide** is a book that gives you information about your destination.

update [V-T-U8] To **update** someone means to tell someone about the most recent news.

warranty [N-COUNT-U3] A **warranty** is the promise from a company to repair or replace an item.

waste time [V PHRASE-U9] To **waste time** means to spend time doing something that is not useful.

wholesale [ADJ-U2] If something is **wholesale**, it is sold in large quantities at a lower price than it would be sold individually in stores.

word-of-mouth recommendation [N PHRASE-U13] A **word of mouth recommendation** is a positive comment about a company between a client and someone who is not yet a client.

Career Paths

Business English

Book 3

John Taylor
Jeff Zeter

Book
3

Express Publishing

Table of Contents

Get ready!

1 Before you read the passage, talk about these questions.

1 What values do you think make a company successful?
2 What traits or actions can discourage customers from doing business with a company?

environmental issues

Software plus
OUR COMPANY'S CORE VALUES...

At Software Plus, we value our customers above all else. We want to:

- provide quality products at **affordable** prices
- keep prices as low as possible so that our customers know they are getting a fair deal
- treat each customer as an individual
- strive to make every person who shops with us feel important and valued

Software Plus also recognizes **innovation** as a key part of our business. We will take steps to:

- stay **one step ahead** of the market
- monitor current **trends** and move quickly to fill **gaps** in the market

The employees of Software Plus are the company's greatest **asset**. As such, we **endeavor** to:

- provide a pleasant, friendly working environment
- supply training **opportunities** and **perks**
- foster professional growth and development

Environmental issues are a **priority** at Software Plus. We promise to:

- support a wide range of environmentally friendly **initiatives**, such as recycling and car sharing
- never knowingly create a product that is harmful to the environment

affordable

Reading

2 🎧 Listen and read this poster about a company's values. Then, read the summary of the text. Fill in the blanks with the correct words from the word bank. How does the company value their customers? Tell the class.

 **BANK**

products   customers   employees
market   opportunities

The company 'Software Plus' has four core values. To begin with, it aims to put **1** _____ first. Secondly, it tries to stay ahead in the **2** _____ by identifying what is popular. Thirdly it treats its **3** _____ well by providing perks and training **4** _____. Finally, it never creates **5** _____ that harm the environment.

Vocabulary

3 Match the words (1-7) with the definitions (A-G).

1 __ gap   5 __ perk
2 __ trend   6 __ opportunity
3 __ innovation   7 __ endeavor
4 __ priority

A a benefit people receive from their jobs
B the most important thing to do
C a new development
D to try to do something
E a temporarily popular item or style
F a place where something is missing
G a chance to do something useful

4 **Read the sentence pairs. Choose where the words best fit in the blanks.**

1 foster / strive

The company aims to _____ the staff's development.

Mr. Gao wants his workers to _____ to do their best.

2 affordable / one step ahead

It's important to stay _____ of our competition.

The other company's product is more _____ .

3 initiatives / core values

This company has three _____: loyalty, quality and trust.

There are many new _____ to help small businesses.

4 environmental issues / assets

The company was forced to sell many of its _____ .

Being aware of _____ can reduce pollution.

Listening

5 🎧 **Listen to a conversation between two managers. Mark the following statements as true (T) or False (F).**

1 __ The poster will be displayed in the break room.

2 __ The man wants to include a statement about current employees.

3 __ The woman thinks people will like the environmental initiatives.

6 🎧 **Listen again and complete the conversation.**

Manager 1:	I need some help with this poster for next month's 1 _____ _____ .
Manager 2:	Sure, have a seat. What can I do?
Manager 1:	Well, management wants a display that shows our 2 _____ _____ . The problem is, the manual lists a lot of values, but I can only show four.
Manager 2:	I'd start with customer care. You could write about how we keep our software affordable.
Manager 1:	That's good, thanks. What do you think of including 3 _____ _____ , though?
Manager 2:	Yeah, why not? You could mention a few of our environmental initiatives. Like our recycling program.
Manager 1:	Good idea. But it's a job fair, and there's 4 _____ _____ _____ _____ _____ . I should include something about them, right?
Manager 2:	What do you 5 _____ _____ _____?

Speaking

7 **With a partner, act out the roles below, based on the dialogue from Task 6. Then switch roles.**

USE LANGUAGE SUCH AS:

I need some help with this poster …

I'd start with …

What do you think of …

Student A: You need to choose four core values for a poster. Talk to Student B about:

● suggestions

● your ideas

● attracting employees

Student B: Answer Student A's questions and make suggestions.

Writing

8 **You are writing a website page about your company's core values. Using the poster and the conversation from Task 7, write a paragraph for the website (100-120 words). Talk about:**

● What your company's core values are

● What your company endeavors to do

● How your company stays one step ahead

2 Business in different cultures

etiquette

eye contact

Get ready!

1 Before you read the passage, talk about these questions.

1 What are some ways people greet each other in formal and informal situations?

2 What are some things foreigners might accidentally do that are offensive in your culture?

◀◀ Conducting Business Overseas

Conducting business overseas is full of **pitfalls**! There are many different customs regarding **etiquette**. You may make a major social **gaffe** without realizing it! This guide outlines the areas where mistakes commonly occur.

Consider how you will address your business associate. It is polite to address someone by their **title** and **surname** in many places.

The handshake is recognized worldwide, but in the States and Britain people generally shake hands only once, when they first meet. Be **aware** that in Japan, it is rude to make **eye contact** when shaking hands, and in many Asian countries it is **customary** to bow.

If you are invited to someone's house, you should take a gift to thank them for their **hospitality**. But be careful! Your choice of gift is very important. **Avoid** giving white flowers in Japan or clocks in China because they symbolize death. Be **conscious** of eating customs. In Europe and the States, you may **offend** your **host** if you leave food on your plate. However, in Asia, a clean plate indicates you are still hungry.

In conclusion, the best way to conduct business internationally is by researching **manners** and customs. Only this way can you ensure that you won't make a terrible social **blunder**!

Reading

2 🎧 Listen and read this guide to business etiquette. Then, choose the correct answers. Say four things you have learned from the text.

1 What should you NOT do when visiting Japan?
 A give your host a gift
 B bow when you meet someone
 C leave food on your plate after a meal
 D look a person in the eyes during an introduction

2 What should business travelers do before doing business other countries?
 A purchase reasonable gifts
 B learn the country's language
 C research the country's etiquette
 D memorize new partner's surnames

gifts

3 According to the passage, when do British people shake hands?
 A when greeting business partners in the morning
 B when first being introduced to someone
 C when accepting a gift
 D when entering someone's house

Vocabulary

3 Choose the word which has the same meaning as the underlined word.

1 Looking his client in the eye when they shook hands was a major gaffe.
 A blunder
 B hospitality
 C host

2 Her manners were typically British.
 A pitfall
 B etiquette
 C hospitality

3 He was conscious that he must leave some food on his plate.
 A aware
 B customary
 C eye contact

4 Choose the correct word pair to fill in the blanks.

1 Mr. Sui thanked his ___ for the wonderful ___ .
   A title – surname B host – hospitality
   C hospitality – pitfall

2 ___ making eye contact because it may ___ the other person.
   A Customary – avoid B Offend – host
   C Avoid – offend

3 It is ___ to call someone by their title and ___ .
   A aware – title B customary – surname
   C avoid – hospitality

4 There are a number of ___ people can fall into such as not using a correct ___ .
   A pitfalls – title B hosts – surname
   C hospitality – eye contact

Listening

5 🎧 Listen to a conversation between two colleagues about a business trip. Mark the following statements as true (T) or false (F).

1 ___ The speakers are taking a trip to Japan together.
2 ___ The woman asks the man to explain parts of Japanese etiquette.
3 ___ The woman plans to purchase a gift before she arrives in Japan.

6 🎧 Listen again and complete the conversation.

Co-worker 2:	I've been reading up on Japanese 1_____ . It's got me worried.
Co-worker 1:	What are you worried about?
Co-worker 2:	It's full of 2_____! I'm scared I'm going to make some terrible social 3_____ .
Co-worker 1:	I'm sure that if you're careful of your 4_____ you'll be fine.
Co-worker 2:	That's not the point. Good manners in Japan are different from manners here. Sometimes they're the complete opposite!
Co-worker 1:	Like what?
Co-worker 2:	Well, here you make 5_____ _____ when you shake hands. In Japan that's rude.
Co-worker 1:	Really? I wasn't 6_____ of that.
Co-worker 2:	And it's 7_____ to give gifts to your hosts, but there are so many gifts that can be offensive!

Speaking

7 With a partner, act out the roles below, based on the dialogue from Task 6. Then switch roles.

USE LANGUAGE SUCH AS:

Are you ready for your business trip?

I'm scared I'm going to …

It's customary to …

Student A: You are going on a business trip to another country. Explain to Student B that you are worried about:
● greeting people
● giving gifts

Student B: Your colleague is going on a business trip abroad and is worried about etiquette. Help Student A plan for his or her trip.

Writing

8 You are writing a guide for business people visiting your country. Using the guide and the conversation from Task 7, write a guide to etiquette (100-120 words). Talk about:

● What is customary for people to do when they greet each other
● What people should be aware of during meals
● What sorts of gifts are appropriate

Should You **Change** Your **Management Style?**

Tom Keanes

A good manager has lots of qualities: **ambition**, drive and the **resourcefulness** to lead a company into the future. But additionally, managers need to decide what relationship they will have with their team-members. Let's review the three major options.

Authoritarian style – Here the manager remains **distant**. He or she makes all the decisions, gives the orders and expects **subordinates** to obey. This style is **limiting**, but is useful when quick decisions need to be made.

Paternalistic style – Here the manager is more approachable and gives workers the chance to **contribute** to decision-making. However, although the manager may **consult** the staff, ultimately, he or she will make all the major decisions.

Democratic style – Here, the manager **empowers** the workers and gives them the **autonomy** to make their own decisions. The advantage of this is that it can improve **morale** and **motivation**, but on the negative side, decision-making is a slow process.

No one of the management styles above is right. Each has its pluses and minuses depending on the nature of the business. However the style you choose can **make or break** your company, so it's worth reassessing your style. It could make your company more productive.

Get ready!

1 Before you read the passage, talk about these questions.

1 What are the qualities of a good manager?
2 What are the qualities of a bad manager?

Reading

2 🎧 Listen and read this blog about management styles. Then, mark the sentences as true (T) or false (F). What styles can a manager adopt? Tell the class.

1 ___ An authoritarian manager gets advice from his workers.
2 ___ Staff members with a paternalistic manager will contribute.
3 ___ Giving workers more independence slows the decision making processes.

Vocabulary

3 Write a word that is similar in meaning to the underlined part.

1 Buying lunch for employees improves <u>their happiness</u>.
_ o _ _ l _

2 The project could <u>lead to the success or failure of the company</u>. m _ _ _   _ r   _ r _ _ _

3 Workers do their best when given some <u>independence</u>.
_ _ t _ _ _ m _

4 <u>Giving the power to make decisions</u> to employees makes them loyal.
e _ _ o _ _ _ i _ _

5 Employees don't approach managers who <u>are removed from the group</u>. d _ _ t _ _ _

6 Being <u>inclusive of all employees' opinions</u> can make employees happy. _ _ m _ _ _ a _ _ c

7 Try to provide employees with <u>the urge to do something well</u>. _ _ _ _ v _ _ i _ _

8 Most employees dislike Mr. Gray's <u>controlling style of management</u>.
a _ _ _ o _ _ _ a _ _ _ _   s _ y _ _

4 Fill in the blanks with the correct words from the word bank.

contributes   subordinates   limiting   ambition
consult   resourcefulness   paternalistic

1 _____ your manager for advice.

2 People with _____ want a better job.

3 Good team morale _____ to productivity.

4 The manager is firm but fair with all of his _____ .

5 Kate's idea is _____ – it would create more problems than it solves.

6 _____ shows someone is practical and creative.

7 Mr. Tek isn't _____, and never involves workers in decisions.

Listening

5 🎧 **Listen to a conversation between a business owner and an employee. Mark the following statements as true (T) or false (F).**

1 ___ The meeting was called to discuss the man's management style.

2 ___ Emailing documents saved the company a lot of money.

3 ___ Employees prefer Mrs. Thomas' democratic style.

6 🎧 **Listen again and complete the conversation.**

Employee:	Well, it's not really a complaint. It's just that Mr. Eggers is so, I don't know, **1** _____ .
Owner:	You mean he's hard to approach?
Employee:	Exactly. And when you do, he doesn't really listen to **2** _____ _____ _____ _____ _____ .
Owner:	Can you give me an example?
Employee:	Sure. Just last week I suggested to him that we email documents instead of printing them. It would **3** _____ _____ _____ _____ _____ . But Mr. Eggers didn't even comment on it.
Owner:	Hmm. Thanks for letting me know. I **4** _____ _____ _____ _____ much for morale, does it?
Employee:	Oh, it's not so bad. In fact, I know everyone really likes Mrs. Thomas' management style.
Owner:	What is it **5** _____ _____ that people like?
Employee:	She listens. She let's us contribute.
Owner:	So she's **6** _____ _____ _____ _____ than Mr. Eggers?

Speaking

7 **With a partner, act out the roles below, based on the dialogue from Task 6. Then switch roles.**

USE LANGUAGE SUCH AS:

Do you have a complaint about one of the managers?

Can you give me an example?

I know everyone really likes …

Student A: Talk to an employee about his or her managers. Ask Student B about:

● complaints

● good management

● examples

Student B: You work at Student A's company. Answer his or her questions. Make up some details for two managers.

Writing

8 **You are a business owner. Write a memo to one of your managers suggesting that he or she adopt a new management style (100-120 words). Talk about:**

● What the employee's complaints about the manager's style are

● Why it is important to change the management style

● Which management style you recommend

● Why you recommend this style

Get the Right Team!

Teams can make or break a project. Some teams **gel** instantly and achieve great things, where others **flop**. So what makes a good team? In the 1970s, Dr. Meredith Belbin observed a number of teams to find out. He identified what separates unsuccessful groups from successful ones. In successful groups, the different team-members adopt one of nine different roles.

The 9 Roles:

The Plant is a **creative** individual who solves problems in **unconventional** ways.

The Monitor Evaluator analyzes options and makes impartial judgements on the practicality of ideas put forward.

The Coordinator is good at focusing on the **objective**, and can **delegate** work appropriately.

The Resource-Investigator is good at reviewing information beyond the focus of the team's work.

Implementers are **practical**. They can plan strategies and carry them out efficiently.

As the project nears completion, Completer Finishers have the patience to **scrutinize** it for errors.

Team workers create a **harmonious** team atmosphere, keeping relationships within the team positive.

Shapers **thrive** on pressure. Their **passion** drives the team forward.

Finally the Specialist provides **in-depth** knowledge of one particular subject.

creative

scrutinize

Get ready!

❶ **Before you read the passage, talk about these questions.**

1 What type of people work well in groups? What type of people do not?

2 Describe a group project you were involved in that did not go well. What happened?

Reading

❷ 🎧 **Listen and read this magazine article about teams. Then, choose the correct answers. What roles can be adopted by members of successful groups? Tell the class.**

1 Which team-member is most likely to discover helpful information for a project?

　A　a Team worker　C　a Resource-Investigator

　B　a Coordinator　D　a Shaper

2 According to the article, which of the following is NOT true?

　A　Team workers have good relationships with others.

　B　Plants are good at coming up with ideas.

　C　Coordinators have strong opinions and feelings.

　D　Completer-Finishers are good at finding mistakes.

3 What can be inferred about Dr. Belbin?

　A　He was a Resource-Investigator.

　B　He studied groups for almost a decade.

　C　He observed groups that were not successful.

　D　He saw the nine roles in his own research team.

Vocabulary

❸ **Write a word that is similar in meaning to the underlined part.**

1 A good team is <u>friendly and works well together</u>.
　_ a _ m _ _ _ _ u s

2 Yolanda does her job <u>quickly and well</u>.
　e _ _ _ c _ _ _ t _ _

3 This project is going to <u>be a disaster</u>.
　_ l _ _

4 Be <u>concerned with facts, not feelings</u>.
　_ _ j _ _ t _ _ _

5 Ms. Kent's methods are <u>unusual, but successful</u>.
　_ n _ _ _ v _ _ t _ _ _ a _

6 A manager must learn to <u>give work to other people</u>.
　_ e _ _ g _ _ _

7 Paul is <u>able to find possible solutions to problems</u>.
　_ r _ _ t _ _ _ l

4 Read the sentence pairs. Choose where the words best fit in the blanks.

1 **creative / in-depth**

John has _____ knowledge of music.

Sally is _____ and enjoys painting and writing.

2 **scrutinize / gel**

_____ this document for errors.

A team needs the right people in order to _____ .

3 **strategy / passion**

Helen has a strong _____ for making music.

Develop a _____ for us to save money.

4 **review / thrive**

Some people _____ under pressure.

Roger will _____ all the current documents.

Listening

5 🎧 Listen to a conversation between managers. Mark the following statements as true (T) or false (F).

1 __ The managers' previous project was successful.

2 __ The man believes the group needs multiple coordinators.

3 __ The woman suggests a team member based on his previous creative work

6 🎧 Listen again and complete the conversation.

Manager 1: I guess that's **1** _____ _____ _____ . We need someone who takes charge. A coordinator.

Manager 2: I agree. But we **2** _____ _____ _____ . We don't need two people arguing over what to do next.

Manager 1: Good call. Let's use Erica.

Manager 2: But Erica tends to be too focused on planning, don't you think?

Manager 1: So we'll **3** _____ _____ _____ _____ someone who can get work done fast.

Manager 2: **4** _____ _____ . What do you think of Robert? He's pretty efficient.

Manager 1: I like him as an implementer, yes. So we have a leader and a hard worker – what else do we need?

Manager 2: **5** _____ _____ _____ a plant. Somebody creative. Our client wants a really attractive page.

Manager 1: You know, Bruce has designed some beautiful pages.

Speaking

7 With a partner, act out the roles below, based on the dialogue from Task 6. Then switch roles.

USE LANGUAGE SUCH AS:

We need to choose our team carefully.

Let's talk about personality types and roles.

We need someone who …

Student A: You are trying to put together a team. Talk to Student B about:

● roles

● personality types

● project needs

Student B: Talk to Student A about the team and suggest members. Make up some team members details.

Writing

8 You are a project manager. Write a memo to your company manager stating who you want in your team (100-120 words). Make up the managers' personal details. Talk about:

● How many people you want

● Which skills are important for your project

● Who you want in your team and why

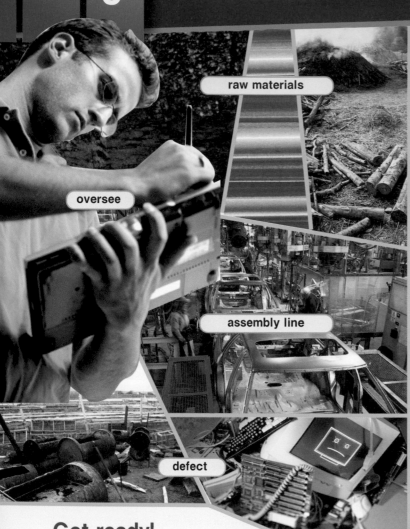

raw materials

oversee

assembly line

defect

PRINGLE AND WEBSTER is currently seeking a
Production Supervisor
$60,000 - $75,000 plus benefits

Pringle and Webster is an established **manufacturer** of stainless steel containers, supplying the dairy and pharmaceutical industries. We currently have five factories in the northwest. We are currently seeking a production supervisor whose primary role will be to **oversee** our **assembly line** and quality control **operations**. This is a full-time post, and is based at our Newcastle plant.

Duties will include:

- Ordering the **raw materials** required for production, ensuring there is minimal **surplus** or shortage
- Ensuring factory **output** levels are maintained
- Checking the final products for defects to ensure there is a minimal level of product **recall**
- **Conferencing** with clients to discuss their design specifications
- Developing **measures** to cut company costs
- Essential - At least three years' experience in a manufacturing environment, working in a supervisory role.
- Ability to meet deadlines
- Desirable - Preference will be given to applicants with experience in **lean manufacturing**. It is hoped that the successful candidate will have a major role in developing and **implementing** new measures such as **just-in-time** production, in order to help the company cut costs and improve the efficiency of production.

conference

Get ready!

1 **Before you read the passage, talk about these questions.**

1 What skills does a supervisor in a manufacturing industry need?

2 Many businesses save money by producing goods in other countries. Has this helped or hurt your country's economy?

Reading

2 🎧 **Listen and read the advertisement for a Production Supervisor position. Then, complete the table using information from the text. Present the job to the class.**

Job Title:	1 _____
Company Name:	2 _____
Manufacturer of:	3 _____
Duties include:	ordering 4 _____ maintaining 5 _____ 6 _____ with clients

Vocabulary

3 **Check (✓) the sentence that uses the underlined part correctly.**

1 __ **A** ZipCo <u>recalled</u> products due to high quality.

__ **B** <u>Conference</u> with the staff for more information.

2 __ **A** There's no need to order more, we have a <u>surplus</u>.

__ **B** Our top quality products have many <u>defects</u>.

3 __ **A** The factory builds <u>raw materials</u> to be sold.

__ **B** Forty employees work on this <u>assembly line</u>.

4 __ **A** <u>Lean manufacturing</u> methods reduce costs.

__ **B** <u>Just-in-time</u> production requires storing.

4 Fill in the blanks with the correct words from the word bank.

Word BANK

operations   output   implement
specifications   manufacturer   oversee

1   Han Inc. will _____ new methods to save money.
2   Check the design _____ before staring production.
3   TamCorp is the biggest _____ of cars.
4   The company must increase _____ to cover increased sales.
5   Mr. Bradley will _____ the workers in the factory.
6   Alice managed quality control _____ at a large factory.

Listening

5 🎧 **Listen to a conversation between an interviewer and an applicant for a job. Check (✓) the qualifications that Mr. Robson already has.**

1   ☐ three years of experience
2   ☐ monitoring quality control
3   ☐ ordering supplies
4   ☐ conferencing with clients
5   ☐ using lean manufacturing

6 🎧 **Listen again and complete the conversation.**

Applicant:	I spent two years with a manufacturer of machine parts.
Interviewer:	What did you do there?
Applicant:	My main role was to **1** _____ the assembly line and keep output levels high.
Interviewer:	Were you involved in **2** _____ _____ ?
Applicant:	Yes. Actually I managed those operations. I'm pleased to say that when I was manager, product recall fell by 37 percent.
Interviewer:	Congratulations, that's impressive. How did you accomplish that?
Applicant:	I **3** _____ _____ _____ _____ _____ measures.
Interviewer:	Well, we're very interested in that type of change. Tell me, were you responsible for any other duties?
Applicant:	Of course. I also had to **4** _____ _____ _____ and avoid shortages.
Interviewer:	And how did you decide what materials to go with?
Applicant:	I just made sure that we **5** _____ _____ _____ our clients wanted.

Speaking

7 **With a partner, act out the roles below, based on the dialogue from Task 6. Then switch roles.**

USE LANGUAGE SUCH AS:

My role was to …
Were you involved in …?
How did you accomplish that?

Student A: You are interviewing Student B for a manufacturing job. Find out if he/she has experience in:

●   quality control
●   overseeing workers
●   conferencing

Student B: You are applying for a job. Answer Student A's questions.

Writing

8 **You are applying for a job in a manufacturing company. Write a covering letter outlining your skills and experience (100-120 words). Make up how long you have worked in manufacturing. Talk about:**

●   How long you have worked in manufacturing
●   What your duties were at your last job
●   What other skills or experience you have

13

6 Marketing

market research

range of products

promotion

memo

Dear Team,

The design stage of our computer gaming console 'Iliad' is nearing completion. Therefore it is time to start planning our marketing strategies. I would like to propose a meeting in three weeks. I've booked the meeting room for 3 o'clock on August 14th. Please let me know if you will be unable to attend.

Please give the following questions some thought before then.

● We are selling to a **niche** market, so what are the characteristics of our **prospective** customers?

● Do we need to do any **market research** to find out which marketing strategies will reach our **target market** most effectively?

● What does our gaming console offer in comparison to the range of consoles sold by our **competitors**?

● Has anyone got any imaginative marketing ideas, besides the usual television commercials, **flyers**, **billboard** ads, Internet etc.?

● What are the best **distribution channels** and **outlets** for our product?
Is it worth exploring new **avenues**?

● What sort of **promotions** will attract **consumers** to our **brand**?

● What type of **packaging** will appeal to our target audience?

I look forward to hearing your suggestions on these issues at the meeting.

Thanks
Bill Turner
PRODUCT DEVELOPMENT MANAGER
ODYSSEY GAMES

Get ready!

① Before you read the passage, talk about these questions.

1 What is the best marketing campaign you can think of? What makes it so good?

2 What qualities would a good marketing employee have?

Reading

② 🎧 Listen and read this memo from a project manager to his marketing team. Then, mark the following statements as true (T) or false (F). Summarise the memo and tell the class.

1 ___ The first attempt to market the 'Iliad' was unsuccessful.

2 ___ Market research has been done to determine the target audience.

3 ___ The company wants to find non-traditional advertising methods.

Vocabulary

③ Choose the correct word pairs to fill in the blanks.

1 Do some _____ to find out what people think of the _____ .
   A competitors – outlets
   B market research – brand
   C target market – range

2 A _____ can encourage _____ to buy things.
   A niche – competitors
   B flyer – avenues
   C promotion – consumers

3 All the products in the _____ have similar _____ .
   A range – packaging
   B outlet – ranges
   C target market – brands

4 Marketing teams try to get a _____ not to buy products from their _____ .
   A target market – competitors
   B distribution channels – flyers   C avenues – outlets

5 The company should distribute _____ in the _____ where its products are sold.
   A billboards – distribution channels
   B flyers – outlets
   C avenues – niches

14

4 Write a word that is similar in meaning to the underlined part.

1 Consider everyone as a <u>possible future</u> client.
p _ _ _ p _ _ _ i _ _

2 This a <u>small, specialized</u> market. _ _ c _ e

3 Advertising on <u>very large boards</u> is inexpensive.
b _ _ _ b _ _ _ _ s

4 We should explore other <u>routes and directions</u>.
_ v _ n _ _ s

5 Get new <u>ways in which products are made available to customers</u>. d _ _ t _ _ b _ t _ _ n c _ _ _ n _ _ s

Listening

5 🎧 Listen to a conversation between two employees. Choose the correct answers.

1 What does the manager believe is good news for the company?
A The price of the product has been lowered.
B Competitors are struggling to sell their products.
C More people are becoming interested in gaming.
D The packaging of the product has been approved.

2 What can you infer about the company?
A It controls a chain of gaming stores.
B It's hired a marketing firm to do research.
C Its niche is composed mostly of teenage girls.
D It has not sold products in supermarkets before.

6 🎧 Listen again and complete the conversation.

Employee:	Not necessarily. My research shows that gaming is a lot more popular with all ages these days. And girls are becoming more interested.
Manager:	That's good news for us.
Employee:	Yeah, and I think that's where our competitors **1** _____ _____ . They mostly target young males.
Manager:	But you think **2** _____ _____ _____ older people and girls.
Employee:	I do. We could widen our niche, **3** _____ _____ _____ .
Manager:	That's a very interesting idea.
Employee:	Of course, it means we may need to explore new avenues for advertising.
Manager:	And I assume we'd need **4** _____ _____ _____ , too.
Employee:	Probably. I thought we might stock the console in supermarkets as well as the usual gaming stores and online outlets.
Manager:	Good thinking. **5** _____ _____ _____ packaging?

Speaking

7 With a partner, act out the roles below, based on the dialogue from Task 6. Then switch roles.

USE LANGUAGE SUCH AS:

I've been thinking a lot about …

My research shows that …

We may need to explore new …

Student A: You are planning the marketing for a new product. Talk to Student B about
● prospective customers
● advertising
● distribution channels

Student B: Talk to Student A about the marketing for a new product. Make up a product and target market.

Writing

8 Imagine that your company is developing a product. Choose a product and write an email to your manager with your marketing ideas (100-120 words). Make up a name for the employee. Talk about:

● Who your prospective consumers are
● What the best way to advertise to them is
● What distribution channels and outlets you would recommend

7 Finance

Get ready!

1 Before you read the passage, talk about these questions.

1 What information might be included in a financial report?

2 Why is it important for a company to keep financial records?

takings

assets

ANNUAL REPORT

profit and loss

Reading

2 🎧 Listen and read this email from the Director of Finance to a CEO. Then, choose the correct answers. Summarise the email. Tell the class.

Dear Mr. Ingol,

Please find enclosed the annual **financial report**. In summary, the **profit and loss** statement shows that we are up $7,658.04 on our **earnings** last year. Our increased earnings were due to the **revenue** received from the Taylor Johnson project. In fact, you will see on the spreadsheet that this one project alone brought in 20% of our annual **income** after **deductions**. Our profit was greatest in the 3rd **quarter**, when we received payment from Taylor Johnson and also received the **grant** from the Environmental Awards Group. Profit was lowest in the first quarter, when the company suffered a **net loss**. However, this was due to the increased **expenditure incurred** when we bought the new delivery vehicles, and there was no actual fall in earnings.

The **balance sheet** shows that value of our **assets** is down this year. This is due to the **depreciation** incurred by our outdated computer system. However, the proposed purchase of a new computer system will result in an increased value in our assets by the end of the next financial year. We also have over $3,000 in **liabilities**.

If you have any questions about the report, please get in touch.

Graham Knowles
Director of Finance

grant

1 Which of the following statements is NOT true?

A The takings are higher than last year.

B Most of the profit came in the second quarter.

C The company received a grant in the third quarter.

D The company bought delivery vehicles in the first quarter.

2 The company's assets decreased in value because

A this year's profits were low.

B the company suffered a net loss.

C the delivery trucks were expensive.

D the computers decreased in value.

3 What is the company likely to do next year?

A buy a new computer system

B receive $3,000 in debts

C receive a grant

D reduce spending

Vocabulary

3 Match the words (1-7) with the definitions (A-G).

1 __ expenditure   5 __ grant

2 __ balance sheet   6 __ net loss

3 __ assets   7 __ financial report

4 __ depreciation

A money given to help a specific project

B a situation where you spend more than you receive

C a document giving information about finances

D the money you spend

E things you own which have value

F the loss in something's value over time

G a document containing statements relating to money

4 Choose the correct word pairs to fill in the blanks.

1 The company's ___ was high, but it owes $5,300 in ___ .
   A revenue – liabilities   B quarter – earnings
   C income – profit and loss

2 The expenditure ___ was greatest in the last ___ .
   A deductions – income   B incurred – quarter
   C liabilities – asset

3 The ___ statement shows that our ___ were higher last year.
   A quarter – deductions   B incurred – net loss
   C profit and loss – earnings

4 Our total ___ increased, not including ___ for raises.
   A financial report – assets   B income – deductions
   C expenditure – depreciation

Listening

5 🎧 **Listen to a conversation between a CEO and a manager. Mark the following statements as true (T) or false (F).**

1 ___ The company suffered a net loss in the last quarter.
2 ___ The company earned income from the Hilton project last month.
3 ___ The man expects losses in the next quarter.

6 🎧 **Listen again and complete the conversation.**

Manager: Okay. Well, 1 _____ is here on the left, and
2 _____ is on the right.

CEO: How do our 3 _____ _____ to last quarter?

Manager: Well, they're up from the last quarter, but we actually suffered a net loss over the three months.

CEO: A loss? Why is that?

Manager: We updated the computer systems. It was pretty expensive.

CEO: Oh yes, of course.

Manager: But I expect us to make a profit in the next quarter. We'll 4 _____ _____ the revenue from the Hilton project.

CEO: And 5 _____ _____ _____ we'll get that small business grant, too.

Manager: It could be a very good quarter for us.

CEO: Could you 6 _____ _____ _____ an estimate for the upcoming quarter? I'd like to show that to the board.

Speaking

7 **With a partner, act out the roles below, based on the dialogue from Task 6. Then switch roles.**

USE LANGUAGE SUCH AS:

Have you completed …

Why is that?

There's no guarantee that …

Student A: You are a CEO. Talk to Student B about:
- financial report
- explanation of report
- next quarter

Student B: You are a financial manager. Answer Student A's questions.

Writing

8 **You are a financial manager. Write a brief memo to the CEO explaining why there was a net loss in the last quarter (100-120 words). Talk about:**

MEMO

- Lower takings last quarter
- Why expenditure was high in the last quarter
- What you expect will happen in the next quarter

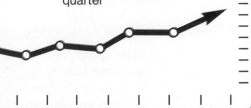

Get ready!

1 Before you read the passage, talk about these questions.

1 What must a salesperson do to ensure a sale?

2 What difficulties might a salesperson encounter when dealing with a client?

pitch

Lucrative SOLUTIONS

Sales Seminar
5-day workshops
tailored to your needs.

In today's competitive market, you need to be sure that your sales team is ahead of the game. That's why we've developed a successful five-day seminar to help organizations like yours to develop a professional and **effective** sales team. Our courses are specially designed to help your sales team **generate** more **appointments**, deliver successful **pitches** and bring in more business. The course covers the entire sales process, from the initial greeting to closing the deal.

During the course you will learn how to:

- Create an effective sales plan to help you set and achieve your sales goals
- **Analyze** your territory and your competitors
- **Capitalize** on opportunities, develop **key contacts** and **influence** the right buyers
- **Approach** potential customers in a **consultative** manner
- Match your sales approach to the personality of your customers
- Become an **attentive** and active listener
- Handle **resistance** and **deal with** negativity
- Maintain your **existing** accounts
- Define and **demonstrate** your strengths and develop new skills

Your sales team will leave the seminar equipped with everything they need to fulfill your clients' real needs. For more information, or to book a course, please telephone 1(800)-555-2718.

www.lucrativesolutions.com

key contact

Reading

2 🎧 Listen and read this flyer advertising a set of seminars for salespeople. Then, read the paraphrase of the article. Fill in the blanks with the correct words from the word bank. What will people learn during the seminar? Tell the class.

seminars   customers   process   business

Lucrative Solutions offers tailor-made courses to salespeople. The aim of the **1** _____ is to help salespeople be more professional and bring in more **2** _____ . The course covers all elements of the sales **3** _____, such as analyzing territory, handling resistance and approaching **4** _____ .

Vocabulary

3 Read the sentence and choose the correct word.

1 The sales team delivered a successful **(approach / pitch)**.

2 Tom's sales approach is not very **(effective / existing)**.

3 **(Capitalize / Analyze)** on this new contact to sell more products.

4 The idea to lower prices met a lot of **(influence / resistance)**.

5 Salespeople use many skills to **(influence / demonstrate)** people.

6 Many salespeople must **(generate / approach)** appointments.

4 Read the sentence pairs. Choose where the words best fit in the blanks.

1 **attentive / consultative**

Be more _____ when you listen to people.

Build a(n) _____ relationship with clients.

2 **deal with / demonstrate**

_____ your skills before an audience.

It's hard to _____ difficult people.

3 **key contact / appointment**

Mr. Robert's _____ is in half an hour.

John is our _____ at that company.

Listening

5 🎧 **Listen to a conversation between a company manager and a sales supervisor. Mark the following as true (T) or false (F).**

1 __ The woman agrees to send the team to the seminar.

2 __ The sales team has lost several important accounts.

3 __ The man wants to hire new salespeople.

6 🎧 **Listen again and complete the conversation.**

Supervisor:	We have some salespeople who haven't **1** _____ _____ _____ in months. Clearly, they need to **2** _____ _____ _____ somehow.
Manager:	Yes, good point. But isn't that something we can do in-house?
Supervisor:	We could try. But I think they would benefit from some practice with other professionals.
Manager:	I see. Well, if you think **3** _____ _____ _____, go ahead. But this **4** _____ _____ some other concerns.
Supervisor:	What's that?
Manager:	I need to know if our **5** _____ _____ can manage our existing accounts.
Supervisor:	Well, some of our key contacts have shown some resistance to our latest sales drives. But we haven't **6** _____ _____ _____ .

Speaking

7 **With a partner, act out the roles below, based on the dialogue from Task 6. Then switch roles.**

USE LANGUAGE SUCH AS:

I think it would benefit our team.

Do you think it's necessary?

Do we need to bring in new personnel?

Student A: A sales supervisor has concerns about the sales team. Talk to Student B about:
- a sales seminar
- pitches and appointments
- new employees

Student B: Talk to Student A about the sales team and seminar.

Writing

8 **You are a sales supervisor. Write an email to the company manager explaining why you believe a sales seminar would benefit your team (100-120 words). Talk about:**

- What the course promises to do
- What the current problems in the sales team are
- Why you think the seminar would benefit your team

specification

certification

Quality STANDARDS

PENN PLASTICS - Employee Manual

At Penn Plastics we take great pride in the quality of our work. As an employee, you will be expected to familiarize yourself with **guidelines** published by the **International Organization for Standardization (ISO)** that apply to our field.

Chapter one in this manual outlines our **policies** regarding standards and **statutory requirements**. We are in compliance with all of the **statutes** regulating our industry and proudly maintain the highest standards.

Because most of our products are made for children, we must follow strict **criteria**, especially when it comes to our **resources** and suppliers. We are ultimately responsible for every product that leaves our factory. It's a responsibility that we take seriously. That's why every employee must complete a course and earn a **certification** in Product Safety.

Our products are designed to meet strict **specifications**. Every employee is expected to keep an eye out for quality control on the factory floor and in the shipping department.

At Penn Plastics, we're like family. We all have a vested interest in what we do and what we produce.
You've joined a great team.

Chapter 4

guideline

criteria

Get ready!

❶ **Before you read the passage, talk about these questions.**

1 Why is it difficult to enforce international manufacturing standards?

2 How do international guidelines impact businesses?

Reading

❷ 🎧 **Listen and read the page from an employee manual. Then, mark the following statements as true (T) or false (F). Give two reasons why someone should join the company.**

1 __ Penn Plastics executives determine regulatory statutes.

2 __ Most Penn Plastics products are intended for adult use.

3 __ All Penn Plastics employees have taken a product safety course.

Vocabulary

❸ **Choose the word that is closest in meaning to the underlined part.**

1 Alan gives the <u>documents that give evidence of achievement</u>.
A certifications B resources C statues

2 The company must comply with the <u>laws and guidelines</u>.
A specifications B certifications
C statutory requirements

3 This manual contains the <u>written rules and guidelines</u>.
A specifications B policies C resources

4 Follow the <u>product requirements</u>.
A certifications B specifications C policies

5 What are the <u>standards that must be used</u> for testing the product?
A statutory requirements B resources C criteria

4 Place a check (✓) next to the response that answers the question.

1 Does she know about the <u>International Organization for Standardization</u>?

  A __ No, she has never traveled abroad.

  B __ Yes, she studied its guidelines at her previous job.

2 Have the employees followed the safety <u>guidelines</u>?

  A __ Yes, their supervisor made sure.

  B __ Yes, we'll have them done next week.

3 Have you read about the new industry <u>standards</u>?

  A __ Yes, I'm going to call a meeting about them.

  B __ Yes, I know the industry hasn't been profitable.

4 What <u>resources</u> does this company use most often?

  A __ It processes a lot of lumber every day.

  B __ It has produced more products every week.

5 What does the <u>statute</u> say about this material?

  A __ It is legal to use in everything except food.

  B __ The company hasn't hired a lawyer yet.

Listening

5 🎧 Listen to a conversation between an instructor and a new employee. Mark the following statements as true (T) or false (F).

1 __ The new employee has not read the ISO guidelines.

2 __ The woman is responsible for ensuring compliance.

3 __ The certification must be renewed every five years.

statute

6 🎧 Listen again and complete the conversation.

Instructor: Just try to **1** _____ _____ _____ _____ that apply to our industry. It addresses plastics in section seven.

Employee: Great, thank you.

Instructor: Any other questions **2** _____ _____ _____ _____?

Employee: Yeah, actually. I'm just working on the assembly line. But I'm responsible for monitoring **3** _____ _____?

Instructor: Actually, that's **4** _____ _____ _____ . Making sure we're in compliance with all regulations, have our permits ...

Employee: But I have to know about it anyway?

Instructor: We find that it **5** _____ _____ _____ _____ if everyone understands what we have to do and why.

Speaking

7 With a partner, act out the roles below, based on the dialogue from Task 6. Then switch roles.

USE LANGUAGE SUCH AS:

Have you had a chance to read ...?

Just try to ...

How long does this certification last?

Student A: You are a product safety instructor. Answer student B's questions.

Student B: You are a new employee. Ask student A about: statutory requirements.

Writing

8 You are a product safety instructor at a manufacturing company. Write a summary of what new employees must learn before becoming certified (100-120 words). Talk about:

- What you need to study
- How you will get your certification
- Why you must learn about these things

21

Get ready!

1 **Before you read the passage, talk about these questions.**

1 In what ways can you compare the success of different companies?

2 How would you improve the efficiency of a business that exists today?

management strategy

bench marking

quality management

Achieving Perfection in Your Business

You've done your homework, done your **benchmarking**, and studied various management **methods**. Think you've found the perfect **management strategy**? Think again.

Consider your **internal benchmarks**. Have you set goals? Have you taken an honest assessment of your strengths and weaknesses? If you have, you're off to a good start. **Quality management** within your company is the key to success.

Look at your **competitive benchmarks** next. Believe me, your competitors are looking at you, too. Achieving perfection means being a leader in your industry. But there's more. Keep an eye on what is going on in other industries. **Functional benchmarks** offer an opportunity for improvements across a variety of industries and organizations. Don't overlook this valuable tool.

Our recent study looked at **best practice** in the field of manufacturing and applied our findings to other industries at random. As far as management goes, we found that the top performers had the skills to be leaders in any industry.

For example, take the **six sigma** strategy, developed by an electronics company. Certainly, it has its **detractors**, but there is great value in the basic system. It also shows that a good business strategy can be beneficial far beyond its original industry.

Top Business Quarterly
Vol. 2 No.4

Reading

2 🎧 **Listen and read the article from a business magazine. Then, read the summary of the dialogue. Fill in the blanks with the correct words and phrases from the word bank. What did you learn from the text?**

management strategy   methods
benchmarks   best practice

According to the article, the key to a good **1**_____ is to use every available tool. **2**_____ should measure owners' businesses, their competitors and even other industries. The **3**_____ followed in other industries may benefit other industries as well. For optimal results, owners should study all available **4**_____ .

Vocabulary

3 **Match the words (1-6) with the definitions (A-F).**

1 __ functional benchmark

2 __ best practice

3 __ internal benchmark

4 __ detractor

5 __ competitive benchmark

6 __ six sigma

A the comparison of practices among companies in the same industry

B the comparison of similar practices within one company

C a highly successful management strategy

D the comparison of similar practices across industries

E a method that consistently shows the best results

F a person who is critical of something

4 Write a word that is similar in meaning to the underlined part.

1 Develop a new <u>strategy for coordinating staff and resources</u>.
m _ _ _ g _ _ _ n t   _ t _ a t _ _ y

2 Conduct a study of <u>the ways business is carried out</u>.
m _ _ _ o d _

3 A system of <u>investigating successful activities improves</u> workflow.
_ _ _ c h _ a _ _ _ n g

4 TechCo is reviewing its <u>management activities that determine quality</u>.
_ _ a l _ _ y   m _ _ a g _ _ _ n t

Listening

5 🎧 Listen to a conversation between a business owner and a manager. Mark the following statements as true (T) or false (F).

1 __ The company's production methods are less expensive than competitors' methods.

2 __ The man wants to apply best practices from one department to another department.

3 __ Internal benchmarks show that the marketing department is the most efficient department.

6 🎧 Listen again and complete the conversation.

Manager: Because we're way more efficient. We spend about a **1** _____ _____ _____ _____ on production. But the bigger companies spend almost twice that.

Owner: I see. They produce more overall, but our methods **2** _____ _____ _____ than theirs.

Manager: Exactly. In fact, the quality management standards on our production line could be applied elsewhere.

Owner: How so?

Manager: I noticed it while **3** _____ _____ _____ . As efficient as our production line is, our marketing department **4** _____ _____ .

Owner: So what are you suggesting?

Manager: We take the production **5** _____ _____ and apply them to the marketing department.

Speaking

7 With a partner, act out the roles below, based on the dialogue from Task 6. Then switch roles.

USE LANGUAGE SUCH AS:

How's that benchmark study coming along?

How can you be sure?

The quality management standards on our …

Student A: You are a manager and you have completed a benchmark study. Talk to Student B about:

● competitive benchmarks

● production methods

● internal benchmarks

Student B: You are a business owner. Talk to Student A about a benchmark study.

Writing

8 You are a manager and you have completed a benchmark study. Write a memo explaining the study to the business owner (100-120 words). Make up names for the owner and the manager. Talk about:

● What the results of the study are

● How you can prove the results

● What you found when examining internal benchmarks

● How the company can improve

Get ready!

1 **Before you read the passage, talk about these questions.**

1 What are some things that can help improve a business's revenue?

2 How can having a successful business strategy help a business?

Reading

2 🎧 **Listen and read the email to a board of directors from a CEO. Then, read the paraphrase of the email. Fill in the blanks using words and phrases from the word bank. Which goals has the CEO in mind?**

 **BANK**

> **dominates** **recognizable** **assets**
> **board of directors** **business strategy**

A company CEO is sending out an email to the
1 _____ because he thinks they need a new
2 _____ . He is concerned because the
company no longer 3 _____ the market.
The CEO has two strategic goals in mind. First, to
stabilize the company's 4 _____, and
secondly, to make the company's name more
5 _____ .

Vocabulary

3 **Choose the correct word pair to fill in the blanks.**

1 With a good ____, a company doesn't have to ____ its position.

   A foothold – dominate

   B strategy – defend

   C strategic goal – formulate

2 Profits have ____ because the company ____ the industry last year.

   A stabilized – dominated

   B dominated – defended

   C formulated – stabilized

3 To become a(n) ____, RogerCorp must gain a(n) ____ in new markets.

   A foothold – strategy

   B strategic goal – resource allocation

   C industry leader – foothold

To:	The Board of Directors
From:	Luigi Quinn, CEO
Date:	May 1
Subject:	Business **Strategy**

Esteemed members of the Board:

I'll make this brief. We need a new business strategy.

Two years ago, we were at the top. We need to **dominate** the market again. If you ask me, we were lazy and allowed our competitors to establish a **foothold** in what was once our field alone. However, they have only begun to enter the market while we have years of experience behind us.

I propose a new **strategic goal** that will increase **profitability** and **defend** our position as the **industry leader**.

Throughout the **planning** stages of this strategy, I have spoken with all of the company vice presidents about the appropriate **resource allocation** to meet our goals.

Stabilizing our assets is goal number one.

Name recognition is goal number two.

We've worked hard to **formulate** a plan. Now we need your support. At tonight's board meeting, I will give a formal proposal with the details of this new strategy. In preparation, please take a few moments to read the attached documents.

Let's move our company right back into the top position.

Sincerely,
Luigi Quinn

4 Check (✓) the sentence that uses the underlined part correctly.

1 __ **A** Ms. Powers <u>formulated</u> a new plan.

 __ **B** <u>Resource allocation</u> involved hiring employees.

2 __ **A** The board voted to remove the <u>strategic goal</u>.

 __ **B** The <u>esteemed</u> businessman has a good reputation.

3 __ **A** The employees need an <u>industry leader</u>.

 __ **B** The new building is still in the <u>planning stage</u>.

Listening

5 🎧 Listen to a conversation between a CEO and a director. Mark the following statements as true (T) or false (F).

1 __ The woman helped create the new strategic goals.

2 __ The woman will attend the meeting tonight.

3 __ The board of directors will vote on the proposal at the next meeting.

6 🎧 Listen again and complete the conversation.

CEO: Yes. This company was at the top of the industry, but we're no longer dominant. That **1** _____ _____ _____ .

Director: I agree completely.

CEO: I'm glad I have your support, Anna. I know the other board members **2** _____ _____ _____ .

Director: The email says that you and the company vice-presidents have **3** _____ _____ _____ to achieve this?

CEO: Yes, we've been **4** _____ _____ _____ for about a month now.

Director: I had **5** _____ _____ that you've been thinking about it that long.

CEO: Well, I wanted to make sure the goals were **6** _____ before presenting them to the board of directors.

Speaking

7 With a partner, act out the roles below, based on the dialogue from Task 6. Then switch roles.

USE LANGUAGE SUCH AS:

I just received your email about …

I know the other board members …

I assume it will have all the details of …

Student A: The CEO thinks that your company needs new goals. Ask Student B about:
● plan to achieve the goals
● when to present plan
● where to find details

Student B: You are the CEO of a company who has a proposal for new strategic goals. Answer Student A's questions. Make up personal details for a Director.

Writing

8 You are a CEO of a company. Make notes that will be used to compose a memo to the board of directors about this evening's meeting (100-120 words). Talk about:

● The time and location of the meeting
● What you are planning to propose at the meeting
● When board members will vote on your proposal

CONTRACTOR'S BID PROPOSAL - ESTIMATE

bid

Get ready!

❶ Before you read the passage, talk about these questions.

1 What are some highly competitive professional fields?

2 Name some things that might give one company an advantage over another.

To: Hewster-Copeland, Inc. Employees
From: Ronald Hewster
Date: March 11th
Re: Framer Associates

Since Framer Associates won the bid for the city's downtown revitalization contract, it has been getting a lot of publicity. That publicity has prompted new clients to seek out Framer Associates' services and its business is **booming**. As a result, it has gone from being a **minor player** to one of our top **competitors**.

While it may seem like Framer Associates is a major **threat** to our company, I do not want any of our employees at Hewster-Copeland to think we are no longer a **key player** in the contracting and construction market. We have the **advantage** – our reputation is solid, and we have spent years building customer loyalty through hard work and dedication. When it comes to experience and trustworthiness, we have the **edge** over Framers.

In addition, we have a good relationship with all of the material suppliers in our area, many of whom are always happy to mention our names and **recommend** our services to new customers. Just because we did not **land** the city **contract** does not mean that we are ruined. In fact, earnings reports show that we still are the top **grossing** contracting and construction firm in the city.

I thank you all for your continued hard work in making Hewster-Copeland the best in the business.

Sincerely,
Ronald Hewster

booming

Reading

❷ 🎧 Listen and read the memo to employees regarding a competing company. Then, mark the following statements as true (T) or false (F). What advantage does Hewster-Copeland have over Framer Associates?

1 __ Hewster-Copeland lost an important contract to Framer Associates.

2 __ Framer Associates had higher profits than Hewster-Copeland.

3 __ Suppliers suggest that people use Hewster-Copeland's services.

Vocabulary

❸ Fill in the blanks with the correct words and phrases from the word bank.

word BANK

| bid | key player | minor player |
| advantage | land | grossing |

1 The company is a _____ in the auto industry.

2 Which company submitted the lowest _____?

3 BeautyCo's line of makeup is its highest _____ product.

4 Ronald's experience gave him a(n) _____ .

5 Mary's small business is just a _____ in the industry.

6 James has been unable to _____ new clients.

4 Match the words (1-6) with the definitions (A-F).

1 __ contract   4 __ edge

2 __ competitor   5 __ recommend

3 __ threat   6 __ boom

A to increase or become more successful

B something that is able to cause damage or hurt

C to suggest

D a quality that helps a company succeed

E an agreement between two companies

F a rival in the same field

Listening

5 🎧 **Listen to a conversation between a manager and an employee. Mark the following statements as true (T) or false (F).**

1 __ Janet is employed by Framer Associates.

2 __ Hewster-Copeland supplies construction materials.

3 __ The man is not concerned about the competition.

6 🎧 **Listen again and complete the conversation.**

Manager: Come on, Janet. **1** ____ ____ ____ .

Employee: It's just some of us are concerned that the company isn't as **2** ____ as it used to be.

Manager: Does this have anything to do with **3** ____ ____ ____ for the city contract?

Employee: Sort of. It just seems like since Framer Associates got the contract, their business has been **4** ____ .

Manager: I can assure you, Janet, that Hewster-Copeland is doing just fine. We actually **5** ____ ____ ____ on Framer Associates.

Employee: We do?

Manager: We've been in this business a long time. Hewster-Copeland has a great **6** ____ in the city.

Employee: That is true.

Manager: And our excellent relationship with our **7** ____ also gives us an advantage.

Speaking

7 **With a partner, act out the roles below, based on the dialogue from Task 6. Then switch roles.**

USE LANGUAGE SUCH AS:

What is it you wanted to talk to me about?

I can assure you …

It's just been alarming to see …

Student A: You are an employee who is concerned about how your company is doing. Ask Student B about:

● the company's strength

● why your company has an advantage

Make up a rival company name.

Student B: An employee wants to talk to you about how your company is doing. Answer Student A's questions. Make up personal details about your employee.

Writing

8 **You are a manager. Write a memo to your employees about your company's competition (100-120 words). Talk about:**

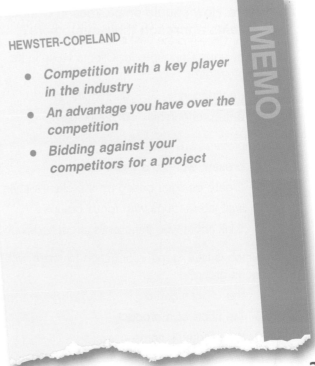

HEWSTER-COPELAND

● *Competition with a key player in the industry*

● *An advantage you have over the competition*

● *Bidding against your competitors for a project*

MEMO

Get ready!

1 **Before you read the passage, talk about these questions.**

1 What are some ways a company can market itself creatively?

2 Some products are marketed at a specific kind of customer. Name some products that are marketed this way and who they market to.

Chapter 1 ● Our Message, Our Model

Employee Manual

Concepts for Clients

At Concepts for Clients, our goal is **innovation**. That's why we have been a leader in the fields of **research and development** (R&D) and marketing for over a decade. You've joined our team because you are an **innovator** and we value your **creativity**.

Our clients are also leaders, when it comes to **entrepreneurship** and business sense. Our promise to them is to create the right marketing plan for their **target audience**. Concepts for Clients has built a solid reputation by consistently fulfilling this promise.

Your **designs** need to reflect our company's style and the wishes of the client. It can be a difficult balance to maintain. Remember, our message is always **optimistic**. Promote our client in a positive way. Steer clear of negative statements about the competition. Think about this question: What is the **incentive** for choosing our client over another company that provides a similar service?

Always show your work to a **focus group** before presenting it to the client. Make sure to keep our client's name **anonymous**. Members of the public are more likely to give an honest opinion that way. For more information on focus groups, see chapter 4.

Reading

2 🎧 **Listen and read the page from an employee manual. Then, choose the correct answers. How should employees in Concepts for Clients approach their customers?**

1 What does Concepts for Clients value in its employees?

  A confidence   **C** imagination

  B entrepreneurship   **D** ambition

2 Employees are advised to

  A present work to a client first

  B create designs based on the client's style

  C limit interactions with focus groups

  D think about who the client's target audience is

3 Which is NOT good information to share with a focus group?

  A the client's name

  B the price of a product

  C the product's name

  D the target audience

Vocabulary

3 **Read the sentence pairs. Choose where the words best fit in the blanks.**

1 **research and development / focus group**

The _____ team thinks the ad will be a success.

The marketing firm asked people to be in a _____ .

2 **innovation / target audience**

The _____ for the product is new homeowners.

Encouraging _____ results in great new products.

3 **design / entrepreneurship**

New business owners must learn about _____ .

The focus group disliked the _____ of the ad campaign.

4 **Fill in the blanks with the correct words from the word bank.**

anonymous   creativity   innovator
optimistic   incentive

1   Don't mention the company name. _____ products get honest opinions.

2   It takes a lot of _____ to design a successful ad campaign.

3   Ms. Barrett is a(n) _____ with fresh ideas.

4   Provide people with a(n) _____ to be loyal.

5   Mr. Ito is _____ that the ad will reach his target audience.

Listening

5 🎧 **Listen to a conversation between a R&D manager and a market researcher. Mark the following statements as true (T) or false (F).**

1   __ The target audience is adults under forty years old.

2   __ Some focus group participants had negative opinions.

3   __ The research and development manager wants a new ad.

6 🎧 **Listen again and complete the conversation.**

Manager: Hi, Grace. How did the **1** _____ _____ for the new Shelbourne ad go?

Researcher: It went well, John.

Manager: Great!

Researcher: But there were some things the **2** _____ didn't like about it.

Manager: Oh ... I thought it was really **3** _____. What didn't they like?

Researcher: Well, the **4** _____ _____ for the product is adults over forty, right?

Manager: Yes, that's right. Most young people wouldn't be interested in that type of **5** _____ .

Researcher: Okay, well, some of them thought the **6** _____ _____ was too edgy ...

Speaking

7 **With a partner, act out the roles below, based on the dialogue from Task 6. Then switch roles.**

USE LANGUAGE SUCH AS:

How did the focus group for ... go?

What didn't they like?

Most young people wouldn't be interested in ...

Student A: You are the manager of R&D. Ask Student B about:

● the focus group

● negative reactions

Make up some personal details.

Student B: You are a market researcher. Answer Student A's questions. Make up some personal details.

Writing

8 **You are a marketing researcher. Write an email to your boss about an ad campaign that was presented to a focus group (100-120 words). Talk about:**

● What the product is

● Who the target audience are

● What they liked and didn't like about the product

Get ready!

1 Before you read the passage, talk about these questions.

1 What are some factors that affect the global economy?

2 Name some aspects of strong economies and weak economies.

Littleton Sun Banner • June 3

The Global Economy and Prosperity

Tonight, economics professor James Murray gave a special lecture on the global economy. He explained that **globalization** has led to higher **economic output** in many places. This, in turn, creates a higher standard of living. In some places, the increase is up to ten percent. Murray says this is because having a global economy allows **developing countries** to trade with **industrialized countries**. As a result, national **debts** can be lowered and consumers can get products at lower prices. Also, workers in countries that engage in global commerce have better paying, higher quality jobs. All these things lead to increased prosperity.

The **gross domestic product (GDP)** of a country increases when it participates in global trade. The expanded **market** requires countries to produce more goods and services. However, the downside is **interdependence**. The daily choices we make, such as which clothes we buy, can actually have an effect on the economy of a country thousands of miles away. Its economy is dependent on what we buy. If a country's trading partner has a **downturn** in its economy, it will affect that country's economy as well.

In conclusion, Professor Murray stated that our economy is no longer solely based on **Wall Street trends**. Instead, the global economy is what will determine our economic situation in the years to come.

●●●

globalization

Reading

2 🎧 Listen and read the following newspaper article. Then, mark the following statements as true (T) or false (F). Summarise the text. Tell the class.

1 __ Globalization has led to a better quality of life in many places.

2 __ Developed countries' debt may increase as they begin global trade.

3 __ Countries are dependent on each other when they engage in global trade.

Vocabulary

3 Match the words (1-7) with the definitions (A-G).

1 __ Wall Street
2 __ trend
3 __ economic output
4 __ prosperity
5 __ developing country
6 __ downturn
7 __ interdependence

A the general way of movement or direction

B an economic state of high income and low unemployment

C a nation that is not industrialized

D the street where the American stock exchange is located

E the amount of goods and services produced

F needing mutual support and assistance

G a decrease in economic activity

4 Check (✓) the sentence that uses the underlined part correctly.

1 ___ A Globalization measures a country's economy.

___ B The company lost money and is in debt.

2 ___ A It's hard to find a gross domestic product in town.

___ B The state of the economy is reflected in the markets.

3 ___ A Industrialized countries often help their poorer neighbors.

___ B People have little money in a period of prosperity.

Listening

5 🎧 Listen to a conversation between a reporter and a speaker on the global economy. Mark the following statements as true (T) or false (F).

1 ___ The man thinks the global economy has more negatives than positives.

2 ___ Companies relocate factories to pay workers lower wages.

3 ___ The woman will use the man's comments in her article.

6 🎧 Listen again and complete the conversation.

Speaker:	Oh, yes. I can spare **1** _____ _____ _____ to talk.
Reporter:	Do you think that your **2** _____ was well received?
Speaker:	Yes, the audience seemed interested in what I had to say about the **3** _____ _____.
Reporter:	And does global commerce always **4** _____ a country?
Speaker:	Well, there are some downsides to globalization. But the good **5** _____ _____ _____ _____.
Reporter:	Can you give me an example of one of the **6** _____?
Speaker:	Well, in some **7** _____ _____ globalization has led to loss of employment.

Speaking

7 With a partner, act out the roles below, based on the dialogue from Task 6. Then switch roles.

USE LANGUAGE SUCH AS:

Do you have a minute?

Well, there are some downsides to ...

Can you give me an example of ...

Student A: You are a reporter. Talk to Student B about:
- the lecture
- effects of globalization
- writing your article

Student B: You are a speaker on the global economy. Answer Student A's questions.

Writing

8 You are a reporter. Using the article and the conversation from Task 7, write down some of the key points mentioned in the lecture for your article (100-120 words). Talk about:
- How globalization affects the world economy
- Why global trade benefits countries
- Why global trade makes countries dependent on each other

Get ready!

1 **Before you read the passage, talk about these questions.**

1 The World Trade Organization regulates international trade. Why is this important?

2 What might happen if there were no regulations for international trade?

WTO (World Trade Organization)

Global Trade Today Blog   *May 15th*

The WTO Debate - When it comes to the **World Trade Organization (WTO)**, there are three kinds of people.

1) The people who support it.
2) The people who don't support it.
3) The people who don't know anything about it.

For those of you who are in the third category, I'll give you a brief explanation. The WTO is an organization that **oversees** global trade. It creates trade laws that govern member nations' companies when they do business. It's also the **venue** for things like negotiating **trade agreements**, settling disputes, and eliminating **trade barriers** like import **quotas**.

Now, why is it so **controversial**? Some people think the WTO has too much power. For example, a member nation's laws cannot **contradict** the WTO's laws. So a nation has to make sure they don't violate the WTO's laws when they want to create a new law. The WTO can also place **trade sanctions** on member countries if they violate a law.

The people who support the WTO say the organization promotes **free trade**. It helps developing countries establish trade with industrialized nations. This **boosts** the economies of all the nations involved. It ensures global business between nations is equal and fair.

What do you think of the WTO? Is it good, bad, or are you undecided? Leave your comments below, but please remember to be respectful of others' opinions.

venue

Reading

2 🎧 **Listen and read the blog post about global trade. Then, mark the following statements as true (T) or false (F). Say three things about the WTO.**

1 ___ The WTO governs the global trade of its members.

2 ___ The WTO's laws are based on the laws of its member nations.

3 ___ Free trade is beneficial for the economies of all nations involved.

Vocabulary

3 **Fill in the blanks with the correct words and phrases from the word bank.**

 BANK

WTO	venue	**quota**	**violated**
	trade barrier	**boosts**	

1 The _____ for the meeting was the conference room.

2 Free trade _____ the economy of countries that export.

3 The leaders eliminated the _____ between the two nations.

4 An import _____ controls trade between nations.

5 The trade negotiations were overseen by the _____ .

6 The company _____ its agreement with its main supplier.

4 Place a check (✓) next to the correct response.

1 Who is <u>overseeing</u> the new project?
   A __ Mr. Leeds will be in charge.
   B __ People who saw it were impressed.

2 Victor made a <u>controversial</u> comment.
   A __ No, Jane apologized for it yesterday.
   B __ Yes, I heard it caused a big argument.

3 Has the <u>trade agreement</u> been finalized?
   A __ Yes, it will take effect in a month.
   B __ No, the country's biggest export is oil.

4 Does this law <u>contradict</u> the old fair trade laws?
   A __ Yes, it will benefit both countries.
   B __ No, it just expands the current regulations.

5 Did the country get a <u>trade sanction</u> put on it?
   A __ The economy has declined since last year.
   B __ The WTO hasn't decided yet.

6 How does <u>free trade</u> help the economy?
   A __ Sellers can get a better price for their goods.
   B __ The trade agreement is not fair to one of the parties.

Listening

5 🎧 Listen to a conversation between a blogger and a co-worker. Mark the following statements as true (T) or false (F).

1 __ The man thinks the WTO is bad for global trade.
2 __ People are protesting the WTO during the conference.
3 __ The woman disagrees with the man's view of the WTO.

6 🎧 Listen again and complete the conversation

M: Aren't they having some kind of meeting in London right now?
W: Yes, it's called a **1** _____ _____ .
M: I thought I saw something on the news about people **2** _____ outside.
W: Well, like I said in my blog … the WTO is **3** _____ .
M: I don't see why. I mean, there needs to be some kind of organization to oversee **4** _____ _____ .
W: Some people think governments should be able to regulate it instead.
M: Yeah, but who's going to regulate the governments when they make **5** _____ _____?
W: Well, other governments could put their own trade **6** _____ on a country that violated any agreements.

Speaking

7 With a partner, act out the roles below, based on the dialogue from Task 6. Then switch roles.

USE LANGUAGE SUCH AS:

Aren't they having some kind of …?

Some people think governments should …

It still seems to me like it's more practical to …

Student A: Talk to a blogger about a recent post. Talk to Student B about:
● the WTO's meeting
● the pros and cons of the WTO

Student B: You wrote a blog post about the WTO. Answer Student A's questions.

Writing

8 You are a blogger. Using the blog and the conversation from Task 7, write notes for a blog post about the WTO (100-120 words). Talk about:

● Where the Ministerial Conference is taking place
● How trade would be regulated if the WTO didn't exist
● The positive things the WTO does for global trade

Glossary

adopt [V-T-U3] To **adopt** something means to start to use it.

advantage [N-COUNT-U12] An **advantage** is a quality or condition that helps a company succeed.

affordable [ADJ-U1] Something that is **affordable** is not too expensive to buy.

ambition [N-COUNT or UNCOUNT-U3] **Ambition** is a strong desire to do something.

analyze [V-T-U8] If you **analyze** something, you study it carefully and draw conclusions from it.

anonymous [ADJ-U13] If something is **anonymous**, its name or identity is not revealed.

appointment [N-COUNT-U8] An **appointment** is a meeting you have already arranged with another person.

approach [V-Tor I-U8] To **approach** means to move nearer to something or someone.

assembly line [N-COUNT-U5] An **assembly line** is a group of machines and people in a factory that work together to build a product.

asset [N-COUNT-U1, U7 & U11] An **asset** is any item of economic value which is owned by a company or individual.

attentive [ADJ-U8] If someone is **attentive**, he cares about the other person's idea and listens carefully.

authoritarian [ADJ-U3] If someone is **authoritarian**, that person makes decisions without consulting others.

autonomy [N-COUNT-U3] **Autonomy** is independence.

avenue [N COUNT-U6] An **avenue** is a route or direction. If you explore different avenues, you think about other ways to achieve your goal.

avoid [V-I-U2] To **avoid** something means to try hard NOT to do it.

aware [ADJ-U2] If you are **aware** of something, you know a little about it.

balance sheet [N-COUNT-U7] A **balance sheet** is a document that shows the value of a company at a point in time.

benchmarking [N-UNCOUNT-U10] **Benchmarking** is a method of investigating successful techniques in an industry and comparing them to one's own business.

best practice [N-COUNT-U10] Methods that consistently show the best results are considered **best practice**.

bid [N-COUNT-U12] A **bid** is a proposal to do a certain job within a certain amount of time and budget.

billboard [N-COUNT-U6] A **billboard** is a large board found in cities and along roads. Companies use them to advertise.

blunder [N-COUNT-U2] A **blunder** is a mistake.

boom [V-I-U12] To **boom** is for something to increase or become more successful.

boost [V-T-U15] To **boost** something is to increase it.

brand [N COUNT-U6] A **brand** is the name and the 'identity' of the product.

capitalize [V-T-U8] If you **capitalize** on something, you use the situation to your own advantage.

certification [N-COUNT-U9] When one earns a **certification** one has a formal qualification in accordance with set standards.

competitive benchmark [N-COUNT-U10] A **competitive benchmark** is a comparison of similar practices among companies in the same industry.

competitor [N-COUNT-U6, U12] A **competitor** is a rival in the same field.

conscious [ADJ-U2] If you are **conscious** of something, you know that it exists.

consult [V-T-U3] To **consult** someone means to ask their opinion.

consultative [ADJ-U8] If you do something in a **consultative** way, you ask questions and find things out, as well as giving information.

consumer [N COUNT-U6] A **consumer** is a person who buys and uses produces sold by someone else.

contract [N-COUNT-U12] A **contract** is an agreement between two companies in which one company agrees to pay the other a certain amount of money in exchange for goods and services.

contradict [V-T-U-15] To **contradict** something is to be inconsistent with something else.

contribute [V-I or T-U3] To **contribute** to a project is to add to its progress.

controversial [ADJ-U15] If something is **controversial**, it causes disagreements or arguments.

core value [N-COUNT-U1] A company's **core values** are good qualities that the company wants to maintain when doing business.

creative [ADJ-U4] If a person is **creative**, that person has lots of good ideas and is often good at art, music or writing.

creativity [N-UNCOUNT-U13] **Creativity** is a characteristic that allows people to think of new ways of doing or making things.

criteria [N-COUNT-U9] Rules, standards and tests used in evaluation and decision making are **criteria**.

customary [ADJ-U2] If it is **customary** to do something, it is normal or usual in that culture.

deal with [V-T-U8] To **deal with** something means to take action to solve a problem.

debt [N-COUNT-U14] **Debt** is the amount of money that a person, company or country owes to others.

deduction [N-COUNT-U7] A **deduction** is an amount you take away from a figure.

defect [N-COUNT-U5] A **defect** is a fault or mistake in a product.

defend [V-U11] To **defend** something is to protect against a challenge or attack.

delegate [V-I or T-U4] To **delegate** work means to give work to other people, according to their skills.

democratic [ADJ-U3] If someone is **democratic**, that person will make sure everyone is involved in making decisions.

demonstrate [V-T or I-U8] To **demonstrate** something means to show and explain it to other people.

depreciation [N-UNCOUNT-U7] **Depreciation** is the loss of something's value over time.

design [N-COUNT-U13] A **design** is a drawing, model or plan for something.

detractor [N-COUNT-U10] A **detractor** is a person who criticizes something.

developing country [N-COUNT-U14] A **developing country** is a nation that is not considered modern or industrialized.

distant [ADJ-U3] If a person is **distant**, that person does not spend a lot of time talking to other people, but prefers to work alone.

distribution channel [N-COUNT-U6] A **distribution channel** is the way you make your product available to customers.

dominate [V-T-U11] To **dominate** something is to control it and have no competition.

downturn [N-COUNT-U14] A **downturn** is a period of time when economic activity is not as strong.

economic output [N-UNCOUNT-U14] **Economic output** is the amount of goods and services produced by a company, region or country.

edge [N-COUNT-U12] An **edge** is a quality or condition that helps a company succeed.

efficiently [ADV-U4] If you do something **efficiently**, you do it quickly and the quality of your work is good.

empower [V-T-U3] To **empower** someone means to give that person the power to make decisions.

endeavor [V-I- U1] To **endeavor** means to work hard in order to do something.

entrepreneurship [N-COUNT-U13] **Entrepreneurship** is the ability and willingness to start and manage a new business.

environmental [ADJ-U1] Something that is **environmental** is connected to protecting the earth and nature.

esteemed [ADJ-U11] If someone is **esteemed**, he or she is respected by others.

etiquette [N-UNCOUNT-U2] **Etiquette** is the rules of good and polite behavior.

Glossary

existing [ADJ-U8] If something is **existing**, it is already there.

expenditure [N-UNCOUNT-U7] Your **expenditure** is the amount of money you spend.

eye contact [N-UNCOUNT-U2] **Eye contact** is the act of looking directly into another person's eyes.

financial report [N COUNT-U7] A **financial report** is a formal record of a business's financial activities.

flop [V-I-U4] To **flop** is to fail.

flyer [N-COUNT-U6] A **flyer** is a piece of paper which advertises your product.

focus group [N-COUNT-U13] A **focus group** is a random selection of people asked to give an opinion on a product or service.

foothold [V-I -U11] A **foothold** is a position that supports a company's further development or expansion.

formulate [V-T-U11] To **formulate** something is to create something.

foster [V-T-U1] To **foster** something means to look after something and help it to grow.

free trade [N-UNCOUNT-U15] **Free trade** is trade between nations without restrictions or fees.

functional benchmark [N-COUNT-U10] A **functional benchmark** is the comparison of similar practices across industries.

gaffe [N-COUNT-U2] A **gaffe** is a mistake in a social situation.

gap [N-COUNT-U1] A **gap** is a space, or a place where nothing exists.

gel [V-I-U4] To **gel** is to work well together and have a friendly relationship.

generate [V-T-U8] If you **generate** something, you make or create it.

globalization [N-UNCOUNT-U14] **Globalization** is the worldwide movement toward interconnected and inter-dependent commerce.

grant [N-COUNT-U7] A **grant** is money that someone gives to help with a specific project.

gross [V-I-U12] To **gross** is to earn a certain amount of money before paying taxes or costs.

gross domestic product (GDP) [N-UNCOUNT-U14] A country's **gross domestic product (GDP)** is the overall output of goods and services produced within the country.

guidelines [N-COUNT-U9] Recommended practices for an industry are called **guidelines**.

harmonious [ADJ-U4] If a group of people is **harmonious**, everyone is friendly and there are no arguments.

hospitality [N-UNCOUNT-U2] **Hospitality** is the act of looking after other people when they visit you.

host [N-COUNT-U2] A **host** is a person who welcomes you when you visit a new place.

incentive [N-COUNT-U13] An **incentive** is a reason for doing or buying something.

income [N-UNCOUNT-U7] **Income** is the money a company receives from sales or investments.

incurred [ADJ-U7] If something is **incurred**, it happens as a result of something else.

in-depth [ADJ-U4] If a person has **in-depth** knowledge, that person knows a lot about a subject.

industrialized country [N-COUNT-U14] An **industrialized country** is a nation that is considered modern, industrialized and financially sound.

industry leader [N-COUNT-U11] An **industry leader** is a company or business entity that has the highest profit or the highest market share.

influence [V-T-U8] If you **influence** someone, you change their mind.

initiative [N-COUNT-U1] An **initiative** is an idea which aims to solve a problem.

innovation [N-COUNT-U1] An **innovation** is a new idea or technology.

innovation [N-COUNT-U13] A business **innovation** is a good idea that can be marketed as a way to make a profit.

innovator [N-COUNT-U13] An **innovator** is a person who is successful at doing new things in his or her field.

interdependence [N-UNCOUNT-U14] **Interdependence** is the act of relying on mutual support or assistance in order to succeed.

internal benchmark [N-COUNT-U10] An **internal benchmark** is the comparison of similar practices within one company.

International Organization for Standardization (ISO) [N-NONCOUNT-U9] The **International Organization for Standardization (ISO)** is an international-standard-setting body composed of representatives from various nations.

issue [N-COUNT-U1] An **issue** is an important matter.

just-in-time [ADJ PHRASE-U5] A **just-in-time** operation aims to provide finished goods at the latest possible time in order to reduce storage costs.

key contact [N-COUNT-U8] A **key contact** is a person in another company who is likely to help you.

key player [N-COUNT-U12] A **key player** is a person or business that is very important and holds a lot of influence.

land [V-T-U12] To **land** something, such as a job, is to be picked to do it.

lean manufacturing [N PHRASE-U5] **Lean manufacturing** is the art of manufacturing goods as cheaply as possible.

liability [N-COUNT-U7] A **liability** is a debt that a company must pay.

liaise [V-T or T-U5] To **liaise** with someone is to talk to them in order to share information.

limiting [ADJ-U3] If something is **limiting**, it has a number of disadvantages that prevent progress.

loss [N-COUNT-U7] A company makes a **loss** when it spends more than it receives.

make or break [V PHRASE-T-U3] If a decision can **make or break** a company, the decision can affect whether the company succeeds or fails.

management strategy [N-COUNT-U10] A company's **management strategy** is the strategy for overseeing and coordinating staff and resources.

manners [PLURAL N-U2] **Manners** are rules of good behavior.

manufacturer [N-COUNT-U5] A **manufacturer** is a person or a company that makes products using raw materials.

market [N-COUNT-U14] A **market** is a real or virtual place where buyers and sellers trade goods, and services.

market research [N-COUNT-U6] **Market research** is the study of what people think of products and services.

methods [N-COUNT-U10] **Methods** are the ways in which a business is carried out.

minor player [N-COUNT-U12] A **minor player** is a person or a business that is not important and does not have a lot of influence.

morale [N-COUNT-U3] **Morale** is the amount of happiness and productiveness in a group of people.

motivation [N-UNCOUNT-U3] **Motivation** is the urge to do something well.

net [ADJ-U7] If something is described as **net**, nothing more needs to be subtracted.

niche [N-COUNT-U6] A **niche** market is a when a company has a small number of specialist customers with particular needs.

objective [ADJ-U4] If a person is **objective**, that person bases decision on facts, not feelings.

offend [V-T-U2] To **offend** someone means to make them feel upset or uncomfortable.

one step ahead [PHRASE-U1] If you are **one step ahead,** your ideas are more up-to-date than those of other people.

operation [N-COUNT-U5] An **operation** is a particular task in a company.

opportunity [N-COUNT-U1] An **opportunity** is a chance to do something desirable or useful.

optimistic [ADJ-U13] If someone is **optimistic**, they are confident that good things will happen.

Glossary

outlet [N-COUNT-U6] An **outlet** is a place that sells products from a particular company.

output [N-COUNT-U5] **Output** is a finished product from an industry.

oversee [V-T-U5, U15] To **oversee** is to supervise someone or something, or to check and supervise a process.

packaging [N UNCOUNT-U6] **Packaging** is the material which holds a product while it is transported and sold. It is often made of cardboard or plastic.

passion [N-UNCOUNT-U4] **Passion** is strong feelings and emotion.

paternalistic [ADJ-U3] If a person is **paternalistic**, he acts like a father towards other people.

perk [N-COUNT-U1] A **perk** is a benefit you receive from your job, such as a company car or gym membership.

pitch [N-COUNT-U8] A **pitch** is a speech or presentation designed to persuade someone to buy something.

pitfall [N-COUNT-U2] A **pitfall** is an unexpected difficulty.

planning [N-COUNT-U11] **Planning** is the management function of forming plans to achieve set goals.

policies [N-COUNT-U9] A company's **policies** are the written rules and guidelines for employee and management practices.

practical [ADJ-U4] If a person is **practical**, that person is good at having realistic ideas to solve problems.

priority [N-COUNT-U1] A **priority** is something that is more important than other things.

profit [N-COUNT-U7] A company's **profit** is the total money it earns after paying the costs of production.

profitability [N-COUNT-U11] **Profitability** is the ability of a company to generate income consistently.

promotion [N COUNT-U6] A **promotion** is a campaign to attract consumers' attention by selling your product at a cheaper price than usual.

prospective [ADJ-U6] A **prospective** customer is someone who is not your customer now, but could be a customer in the future.

prosperity [N-UNCOUNT-U14] **Prosperity** is an economic state of high income and low unemployment.

quality management [N-UNCOUNT-U10] **Quality management** includes all management activities involved in determining quality policy.

quarter [N-COUNT-U7] A **quarter** is a period of three months.

quotas [N-COUNT-U15] **Quotas** are limits on quantities that cannot be legally exceeded.

range [N-COUNT-U6] A **range** is a group of things or products which are part of a set.

raw material [N-COUNT-U5] **Raw material** is a natural product, such as wood or oil. It has not been made into another product.

recall [N-COUNT-U5] A **recall** is the process of returning faulty goods to a company.

recommend [V-T-U12] To **recommend** somebody for something is to suggest that somebody is capable of doing something well.

research and development [N-COUNT-U13] **Research and development** is the field that applies research to solve problems or create new business methods or products.

resistance [N-UNCOUNT-U8] You meet with **resistance** when you meet people who do not want the same things as you.

resource allocation [N-COUNT-U11] **Resource allocation** is the process of dividing resources among projects, departments, etc.

resourcefulness [N-UNCOUNT-U3] **Resourcefulness** is the ability to think creatively and make your own decisions.

resources [N-COUNT-U9] The natural or man-made materials used in manufacturing are called **resources**.

revenue [N-UNCOUNT-U7] **Revenue** is the money that a company receives from its customers.

review [V-T-U4] To **review** something means to study it.

scrutinize [V-T-U4] To **scrutinize** something is to look at it very closely.

six sigma [N-UNCOUNT-U10] **Six sigma** is a highly successful management strategy developed by an electronics company.

specification [N-COUNT-U5] A **specification** is a paper which shows the exact details of a plan or proposal.

specifications [N-COUNT-U9] **Specifications** are the specific requirements to be satisfied by a material or product.

standards [N-COUNT-U9] **Standards** are the written definitions or rules approved by an official or professional agency.

statute [N-COUNT-U9] A **statute** is an official rule established through treaties, national or local standards.

statutory requirements [N-COUNT-U9] The licenses, permits, etc. necessary to carry out a business are the **statutory requirements**.

strategic goal [N-COUNT-U11] A **strategic goal** is a goal specifically designed to impact a company or its economic position favorably.

strategy [N-COUNT-U4, U11] A **strategy** is the plan of action toward a desired goal.

strive [V-I-U1] To **strive** means to try very hard.

subordinate [N-COUNT-U3] A **subordinate** is a person who works at a lower rank than you.

surname [N-COUNT-U2] A **surname** is your family name.

surplus [N-COUNT-U5] A **surplus** is a group of materials which you bought, but you not do not need.

takings [N-COUNT-U7] A company's **takings** are the total money the company receives from clients and customers.

target audience [N-COUNT-U13] A **target audience** for a product is defined by characteristics such as age and income level that make up that group.

target market [N-COUNT-U6] A **target market** is a group of people who you think you can sell your product to.

threat [N-COUNT-U12] A **threat** is something that is able to cause damage or hurt a company.

thrive [V-I-U4] To **thrive** is to do very well.

title [N-COUNT-U2] A **title** is part of your name that shows your social position, rank or achievement, such as Mister, Doctor or Professor.

trade agreement [N-COUNT-U15] A **trade agreement** is a contract that establishes the rules for doing business between two countries.

trade barrier [N-COUNT-U15] A **trade barrier** is a government imposed restriction on free trade.

trade sanction [N-COUNT-U15] A **trade sanction** is a punishment imposed on a country that violates trade agreements or laws.

trend [N-COUNT-U1] A **trend** is a change in fashions or opinions.

trend [N-COUNT-U14] A **trend** is the general way of movement or direction.

unconventional [ADJ-U4] If a person is **unconventional**, that person does things in a different way from other people.

venue [N-COUNT-U15] A **venue** is a place where something happens.

violate [V-T-U15] To **violate** is to not act properly according to a contract, law, or agreement

Wall Street [N-COUNT-U14] **Wall Street** is the street in New York City where the American stock exchange is located.

World Trade Organization (WTO) [N-UNCOUNT-U15] The **World Trade Organization (WTO)** deals with the regulation, negotiation and formalization of trade agreements between participating nations.